Tort Law

Second Edition

Cavendish
Publishing
Limited

London • Sydney

Second edition first published 1999 by Cavendish Publishing Limited, The Glass House, Wharton Street, London WC1X 9PX, United Kingdom

Telephone: +44 (0) 20 7278 8000

Facsimile: +44 (0) 20 7278 8080

E-mail: info@cavendishpublishing.com

Visit our Home Page on http://www.cavendishpublishing.com

British Library Cataloguing in Publication Data

Tort – 2nd ed – (Cavendish law cards)

1 Torts – England   2 Torts – Wales

344.4'2'03

ISBN 1 85941 503 2

Printed and bound in Great Britain

Contents

1 Negligence

Duty of care

Duty situations

The tests for determining the existence of a duty of care have changed. Prior to 1932, there were numerous incidents of liability for negligence but there was no connecting principle formulated which could be regarded as the basis of all of them. These were referred to as 'duty situations'.

The neighbour principle

The first attempt to create a rationale for all the discrete duty situations was made by Brett MR in *Heaven v Pender* (1883) but the most important formulation of a general principle is that of Lord Atkin in *Donoghue v Stevenson* (1932). This is known as the 'neighbour principle'.

> You must take reasonable care to avoid acts or omissions which you can reasonably foresee are likely to injure your neighbour. Who, then, in law is my neighbour? The answer seems to be – persons who are so closely and directly affected by my act that I ought reasonably to have them in contemplation as being so affected when I am directing my mind to the acts or omissions which are called into question.

The 'two stage' test

The 'neighbour principle' is a test based on reasonable foresight and is unquestionably too wide. It needed further refining.

In the 1970s, there were attempts to extend it by defining it as a general principle. In *Home Office v Dorset Yacht Co Ltd*

(1970), Lord Reid said, '[the neighbour principle] ought to apply unless there is some justification or valid explanation for its exclusion'. This lead to Lord Wilberforce's 'two stage' test in the case of *Anns v Merton LBC* (1978).

> First, one has to ask whether … there is a sufficient relationship of proximity … in which case a *prima facie* duty arises. Secondly, if the first question is answered affirmatively, it is necessary to consider whether there are any policy considerations which ought to negative, or to reduce or limit the scope of the duty.

The 'three stage' test

Lord Wilberforce's general principle soon came in for heavy criticism. This began with Lord Keith in *Governors of the Peabody Donation Fund v Sir Lindsay Parkinson & Co Ltd* (1985) when he said that, in addition to proximity, the court must decide whether it is 'fair, just and reasonable' to impose a duty of care.

The case of *Murphy v Brentwood DC* (1991) marked the death knell for the 'two stage' test by overruling *Anns*. *Murphy* talked of adopting an 'incremental' approach to determining the existence of a duty of care. Following the case of *Caparo Industries plc v Dickman* (1990), it is now fashionable to talk of a 'three stage' test, with the following criteria being taken into account:

- reasonable foreseeability;

- proximity;

- 'fair, just and reasonable'.

The reaction against the 'two stage' test was primarily focused on the fact that it created a massive extension to the tort of negligence. The 'incremental' approach avoids such an increase; instead, the tort of negligence is developed by analogy with existing cases. Any novel type of situation would have to show that it is analogous to an existing situation where a duty is owed. This has lead some to argue that the wheel has turned full circle and that there is now a return to 'duty situations'.

There is also a view that the 'three stage' test and the 'incremental' approach are two different tests. The courts have left the situation confused as to which test is to be used and cases such as *Caparo* are authority for both the 'three stage' test and the 'incremental' approach.

Policy considerations

Policy plays a vital role in determining the existence of a duty of care. It can be defined as the departure from established legal principle for pragmatic purposes. Cases such as *Donoghue v Stevenson* and *Anns* consider policy expressly, whereas the approach followed in *Caparo* and *Murphy* is to impliedly consider policy and merge it in to other considerations such as 'proximity' and whether it is 'fair, just and reasonable' to impose a duty.

What issues of policy are commonly raised?

(1) To allow an action would open the 'floodgates' and expose the defendant to an indeterminate liability.

The courts are always keen to limit liability to a determinate amount to a determinate class of persons. For example, in *Weller & Co v Foot and Mouth Disease Research Institute* (1966), the plaintiffs were auctioneers who lost money on account of being unable to hold their auctions as a result of the defendant's negligence in allowing the foot and mouth virus to escape, which lead to restrictions on the movement of cattle. It was said by the court that their damage was 'foreseeable' but so was the damage to 'countless other enterprises'. It would have been equally foreseeable that cafes, newsagents etc in the market town would also lose money. The burden on one pair of defendant's shoulders would be insupportable and policy had to act to limit liability.

(2) The imposition of a duty would prevent the defendant from doing his job properly.

This leads to a class of what have been termed 'protected parties' – persons who enjoy immunity from suit:

* judges and witnesses in judicial proceedings enjoy immunity on grounds of 'public policy';

* barristers; it was held in *Rondel v Worsley* (1969) that barristers were immune from civil action. It was further held in *Saif Ali v Sydney Mitchell and Co* (1980) that the immunity extended to pre-trial work. In *Kelley v Corston* (1997), the defendant who was a barrister advised the plaintiff to compromise a claim for ancillary relief in divorce proceedings. The court later confirmed the settlement as a consent order. The plaintiff subsequently sued the defendant on the basis of negligent advice. The Court of Appeal held that the plaintiff's claim fell within the immunity extended to advocates;

* solicitors enjoy immunity when acting as advocates;

There is a public policy immunity for the carrying out of public duties by public bodies, unless that public body has assumed a responsibility to the individual. It is thought that, to impose a duty, in this situation, would interfere with the way in which public bodies carry out their tasks. The immunity originates with the case of *Hill v Chief Constable of West Yorkshire* (1989). The mother of the last victim of the Yorkshire Ripper sought to sue the police for negligence in failing to apprehend him earlier. There was found to be no special relationship between the police and the victim and consequently no duty could arise. It was felt that to impose a duty would be damaging to police operations. They would deploy their resources defensively on the basis of how they could best avoid civil liability, rather than on the basis of their professional judgment.

The immunity was even held to apply in the case of *Osman v Ferguson* (1992), even where it was known to the police that the plaintiff was being harassed by an identified individual. A school teacher had become obsessed with one of his pupils. He had threatened to do a 'thing like the Hungerford massacre' because of the obsession. Complaints had been made by the plaintiff's family to the police. The same individual eventually shot and injured the plaintiff and also killed his father but there was no duty on grounds of public policy immunity.

However, the police may be liable where there is a special relationship between the police and an informant (*Swinney v Chief Constable of Northumbria Police* (1996)). The police do not have a blanket immunity; there are other considerations of public policy which also carry weight. Hirst LJ gave examples such as the need to protect springs of information, to protect informers, and to encourage them to come forward without an undue fear of the risk that their identity will become known to the suspect or to his associates. The facts of the case were that the plaintiff passed on to the police certain information concerning the unlawful killing of a police officer. The suspect was known to be violent. The informant requested that contact with her be made in confidence. The document containing the information supplied, together with the informant's name, was left in an unattended police car. The vehicle was broken into and the suspect obtained the document. It was arguable that a special relationship existed. But, in *Swinner v Chief Constable of Northumbria (No 2)* (1999), it was held that a duty of care was owed to an informant to take reasonable steps to preserve his confidentiality. However, in the circumstances, there had been no *breach* of that duty.

In the absence of such exceptional circumstances, an immunity did not arise in *Welton v North Cornwall District Council* (1996). An environmental health officer, acting on behalf of a local authority, negligently required the owner of food premises to undertake extensive works to comply with the Food Act 1990. It was argued that the officer exercised a police or quasi-police function and there should be an immunity. This was rejected as the officer had assumed responsibility and, hence, a duty of care was owed.

The same public policy immunity for the discharge of public duties, unless responsibility had exceptionally been assumed to a particular defendant also applies to the Crown Prosecution Service (*Elguzouli-Daf v Commissioner of Police of the Metropolis* (1994)) and the fire brigade (*Church of Jesus Christ of Latter Day Saints (Great Britain) v Yorkshire Fire and Civil Defence Authority* (1996); *John Munroe (Acrylics) Ltd v London Fire and Civil Defence Authority* (1996); *Nelson Holdings Ltd v British Gas plc* (1996)). However, a distinction was made between a positive act of negligence for which there would be liability on the part of the fire brigade and a negligent omission for which there would be no liability in *Capital Counties plc v Hampshire County Council* (1996). A fire officer at the scene of the accident had ordered that a sprinkler system be switched off in a burning building. The result was the fire spread and caused more damage.

In *Harris v Evans* (1998), it was held that the inspector of the Health and Safety Executive did not owe a duty of care to the owner of a business when making recommendations as to whether a particular activity should be authorised under the Health and Safety at Work Act 1974.

The public policy immunities have recently been scrutinised by the European Court of Human Rights in *Osman v UK* (1998). A challenge was made under Arts 2, 6 and 8 of the European Convention on Human Rights. The case arose out of the facts in the case of *Osman v Ferguson* (see above). Article 2 protects right to life; Art 6 protects the right to justice and Art 8 provides for respect for private and family life. There was held to be no breach of Art 2 as the State was not in breach of its positive obligation to take preventative measures to protect an individual whose life was at risk from another. The police did not know or ought to have known that there was a threat to life. For similar reasons, there was no breach of Art 8.

There was a breach of Art 6(1). The exclusionary rule which prevented a full hearing of the applicant's case laid down in *Hill* constituted a disproportionate interference with a person's right to have a determination on the merits of an action and prevented the court from considering competing interests.

(3) It is against public policy to claim that you should not have been born: *McKay v Essex Area Health Authority* (1982).

(4) The courts will not impose a duty where there is an alternative system of compensation: *Hill v Chief Constable of West Yorkshire* – where compensation was payable under the Criminal Injuries Compensation Scheme.

(5) Constitutional relationship between Parliament and the courts. The courts are reluctant to impose a duty where none existed before, as they see this as the constitutional role of Parliament. See Brook LJ in *Hunter v British Coal Corporation* (1998).

The issue of the existence of a duty will only arise in novel cases or where it is sought to overrule an existing precedent against liability. This is referred to as a 'notional duty' and looks at the question from an abstract level. In most cases it will be a question of fact, whether the defendant owes the plaintiff a duty of care on the particular facts of the case. This is referred to as a 'duty in fact'. The existence of that particular duty is not in issue; what is in issue is whether a duty is owed in that particular case. See *Bourhill v Young* (1943), where it was held that the plaintiff was not foreseeable.

Particular aspects of the duty of care

Physical injury
The meaning of the term 'proximity' varies according to who is using the term, when it is being used and the type of injury that has been suffered. As far as physical injury is concerned, the courts will readily hold the parties to be proximate and for this type of injury proximity really equates to foreseeability. In examination questions where the problem revolves around physical injury, it is unlikely that the examiner is requiring detailed consideration of the tests required for a duty of care but the problem will revolve around some other aspect of negligence.

However, the House of Lords has held in *Marc Rich & Co AG v Bishop Rock Marine Co Ltd* (1995) that, even in cases of physical damage, the court had to consider not only

Stages of negligence

Duty of care
Three stage test

(1) reasonable foreseeability
(2) proximity
(3) fair, just and reasonable

Has there been a breach of duty?
Depends on circumstances but the
following are taken into account:
- magnitude of risk
- seriousness of harm
- practicability of precautions
- standard practice but not obvious
  folly

Did the breach of duty *cause* the
injury?
Initially apply 'but for' test.
Was the cause the probable cause of
the injury (*Wilsher*).

Is the damage too remote?
Two competing tests:
- direct consequences (*Re Polemis*
  (1921); *Page v Smith* (1995))

- reasonably foreseeable damage
  (*The Wagon Mound (No 2)* (1967))

foreseeability and proximity but also whether it was fair, just and reasonable to impose a duty.

The third requirement of 'fair, just and reasonableness' was lacking in *Mulcahy v Ministry of Defence* (1996). The plaintiff was a soldier serving with the British army in the Gulf War. He was injured and his hearing was affected when his gun commander negligently ordered a gun to be fired. Two of the components of a duty of care – foreseeability and proximity – were found to be present. However, taking into account the circumstances including the position and role of the alleged tortfeasor and relevant policy considerations, it was not fair, just and reasonable to impose a duty.

An unusual case of negligence causing physical injury is *Revill v Newberry* (1995). The plaintiff, who was a trespasser and engaged in criminal activities was attempting to break into a brick shed on the defendant's allotment. The defendant poked a shotgun through a small hole in the door and fired, injuring the plaintiff. The defendant was found to be negligent and had exceeded the level of violence justified in self defence. The plaintiff, however, was found to be two thirds contributorily negligent.

In the *Marc Rich* case, Lord Steyn drew a distinction between 'directly inflicted physical loss' and 'indirectly inflicted physical loss'. He said that the law would more readily impose liability for the former than for the latter. The defendants unsuccessfully attempted to rely on this distinction in *Perrett v Collins* (1998). One of the defendants had inspected a light aircraft and certified that it was airworthy. The other defendant was the certifying authority. They were held to owe a duty of care to the plaintiff who was a passenger injured in a test flight. The Court of Appeal said that the distinction was more relevant to economic loss and was not germane to physical injury. The test would be applied in novel categories and did not apply to established categories of liability for personal injury.

Rescuers

Rescuers as plaintiff
The law does not oblige a person to undertake a rescue, unless they are in a special relationship, but the courts are favourably disposed to someone who does attempt a rescue and is injured in the process. Like physical injury, the courts require very little more than foreseeability before they hold the parties proximate.

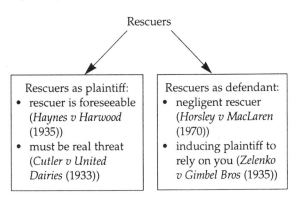

The courts have held that where the defendant has negligently created a situation of danger, it is foreseeable that someone will attempt a rescue and it will not be possible for the defendant to argue that the rescuer is *volenti non fit injuria* or constitutes a *novus actus interveniens*: *Haynes v Harwood* (1935); *Baker v TE Hopkins & Son Ltd* (1959).

As far as rescuers are concerned, the courts are quick to regard someone as being foreseeable and impose few conditions in declaring the parties proximate. However, there must be a real threat of danger: *Cutler v United Dairies (London) Ltd* (1933). The plaintiff attempted a rescue when no one was in a situation of danger and was consequently not owed a duty.

However, even if the victim was not in actual danger, the defendant will owe a duty if the rescuer's perception of danger was a reasonable one: *Ould v Butler's Wharf Ltd* (1953).

The duty owed to a rescuer is independent from that owed to the accident victim. The defendant may, therefore, owe a duty to the rescuer where none is owed to the accident victim: *Videan v British Transport Commission* (1963).

If someone negligently imperils himself or his property, it is foreseeable that there may be an attempt at a rescue and a duty of care will arise on the part of the accident victim. This includes a duty of care to a professional rescuer, such as a fire-fighter (*Ogwo v Taylor* (1987)).

Professional rescuers were also the subject of *Frost v Chief Constable of South Yorkshire Police* (1996). The case arose out of the Hillsborough disaster. The plaintiffs were police officers, four of whom were at the ground at the time of the tragedy but their roles differed. Three of the four were found to be rescuers. A fifth officer who was not on duty at the ground but reported to a hospital later in the afternoon and helped in mortuary duties was not found to be a rescuer and her claim was dismissed. All five officers had suffered post traumatic stress disorder and claimed nervous shock. Relatives' claims for nervous shock damages had been dismissed in *Alcock v Chief Constable of South Yorkshire*

(1992). Despite the fact that both cases arise out of the same incident, the four officers who were present at the ground succeeded in *Frost*. The three officers who were classed as rescuers were owed a duty in two capacities. In their first capacity as rescuers and in their second capacity as employees of the defendant. The fourth officer present at the ground was owed a duty as he was the defendant's employee.

In *Duncan v British Coal Corporation* (1997), the plaintiff was 275 metres from a colleague when he was crushed to death. He was contacted over the telephone and arrived at the scene of the accident within four minutes and administered first aid. He was held not to be a rescuer. See, also, *Kent v Griffith, Roberts and London Ambulance Service* (CA) (1999).

Rescuers as defendant
Although rescuers are quickly held to be owed a duty, there are situations where a rescuer himself can owe a duty to the accident victim:

(1) Where the rescuer by his conduct in commencing a rescue deters or prevents others from attempting a rescue, on the principle of 'detrimental reliance': *Zelenko v Gimbel Bros* (1935).

(2) There is Canadian authority for saying that where a rescuer worsens the condition of the accident victim, then the rescuer becomes liable to the accident victim: *Horsley v MacLaren* (1970).

(3) There is no duty at large to help someone in need of urgent assistance. However, when an ambulance service accepts a 999 call, a duty will be owed if the patient is identified by name and address.

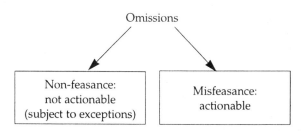

The law makes a distinction between misfeasance and nonfeasance. There is liability for the former but not for the latter. In other words, there is no liability for omissions. A can watch B drown in an inch of water and incur no legal liability, unless A stands in a special relationship to B. However, if you start off a chain of events and then omit to do something, for example, begin driving a car and then omit to brake, with the result that you knock someone down, then there will be liability.

Liability for acts of third parties

Similarly, you cannot be held liable for the acts of third parties, unless there is a special relationship with that third party. In *P Perl (Exporters) Ltd v Camden LBC* (1984), thieves gained entry into the defendant's flat and then were able to break into the plaintiff's property. It was accepted that the damage was foreseeable but there was no obligation on the part of the defendants to prevent the harm from occurring. *Perl* was followed in the case of *King v Liverpool City Council* (1986). In this case, the defendants left their property vacant and unprotected, with the result that vandals gained entrance damaging the plaintiff's flat. The defendants were held not to be responsible for the acts of the vandals. What particularly troubled the court was the question of what would be the extent of the defendant's obligation if he was obliged to protect his property. Would it have to be put under 24 hour guard, etc?

In *Smith v Littlewoods Organisation Ltd* (1987), it was held that the defendant could be responsible for the acts of third parties if 'special circumstances' existed as follows:

- 'special relationship' between plaintiff and defendant;

- source of danger negligently created by the defendant and reasonably foreseeable that third parties would interfere;

- the defendant had knowledge or means of knowledge that a third party had created or was creating a risk of danger on his property and failed to take reasonable steps to abate it.

On the facts of *Littlewoods*, the damage was not reasonably foreseeable, so the defendants were not liable. There was a difference in approach between the judges in *Littlewoods*; Lord Goff saw the intervention of a third party as a *novus actus interveniens* which 'breaks the chain of causation'. On the other hand, Lord Mackay did not see the question in terms of remoteness and causation but in terms of fault. He felt that a third party intervention does not absolve the defendant from liability but, in most cases, the chances of harm being caused by a third party is slim, therefore, it is not reasonable to expect the defendant to take precautions against the harm occurring.

Lord Goff's view is the preferred by most academic writers and was followed by the Court of Appeal in *Topp v London Country Bus (South West) Ltd* (1993). An employee of the

defendant bus company habitually left his bus unlocked
with the key in the ignition. After a short interval, a relief
driver would drive the bus away. On the day in question,
the relief driver failed to turn up and some time later the bus
was stolen by joy riders who knocked down and killed the
plaintiff's wife. The Court of Appeal held that no duty of
care arose. Arguably, if Lord Mackay's test had been used,
then the plaintiff would have succeeded as the trial judge
had found the defendant's actions to be careless.

Nervous shock or psychiatric injury

Types of claimant in nervous shock cases

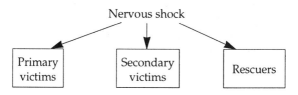

The courts have been slow to allow claims for nervous
shock unless they are coupled with physical injury to the
plaintiff. There are many criteria that the plaintiff must
satisfy before there is liability for nervous shock.

Nervous shock

	Primary victim	Secondary victim
what is regarded as being foreseeable?	physical injury, psychiatric injury need not be foreseen	psychiatric injury
policy limitations	no	yes

Primary victims

The law of negligence relating to nervous shock makes an important distinction between primary and secondary victims. Primary victims are those which have been directly involved in the accident and are within the range of foreseeable physical injury. In the case of secondary victims who are not within the range of foreseeable physical injury, certain control mechanisms are put in place to limit the number of claimants to avoid an opening of the floodgates. These principles are derived from a decision by the House of Lords in *Page v Smith* (1995). The plaintiff suffered from *myalgic encephalomyelitis*, also known as chronic fatigue syndrome or post viral fatigue syndrome. In the eyes of the law, this is regarded as a psychiatric injury. The plaintiff was physically uninjured in a collision between his car and a car driven by the defendant but his condition became chronic and permanent, as a result of the accident. Secondary victims are required to show that injury by way of nervous shock had to be foreseeable (*Bourhill v Young* (1943); *King v Phillips* (1953)).

In *Page v Smith*, the collision was relatively minor and nervous shock was not foreseeable. Nevertheless, the plaintiff recovered as a result of the foreseeability of physical injury, even though the plaintiff was not actually physically injured. Lord Lloyd felt that to inquire whether the plaintiff was actually physically injured introduces hindsight into the question of foreseeability, which has no part to play with primary victims. However, hindsight was a legitimate consideration with secondary victims. Lord Lloyd also felt that there was no justification for introducing a distinction between physical and psychiatric illness, at least as far as primary victims are concerned.

Policy limitations in case of secondary nervous shock victims

```
┌─────────────────────────────────────────────┐
│        Recognisable medical condition        │
└─────────────────────────────────────────────┘
┌─────────────────────────────────────────────┐
│  Proximity in terms of time and space:       │
│  • at scene of accident                      │
│  • in vicinity of accident                   │
│  • came across immediate aftermath           │
└─────────────────────────────────────────────┘
┌─────────────────────────────────────────────┐
│  Proximity in terms of relationship:         │
│  close and loving relationship               │
└─────────────────────────────────────────────┘
┌─────────────────────────────────────────────┐
│       Psychiatric injury is foreseeable      │
└─────────────────────────────────────────────┘
┌─────────────────────────────────────────────┐
│              Normal fortitude                │
└─────────────────────────────────────────────┘
┌─────────────────────────────────────────────┐
│       Perceived accident with own            │
│             unaided senses                   │
└─────────────────────────────────────────────┘
┌─────────────────────────────────────────────┐
│              Sudden trauma                   │
└─────────────────────────────────────────────┘
```

Lord Keith, in a dissenting judgment, felt that the injury had to belong to a class or character that was foreseeable.

Rescuers and employees were classed as primary victims in *Frost v Chief Constable of South Yorkshire* (1996). It was held in *White v Chief Constable of South Yorkshire* (1999) that an employer is not under an obligation to protect employees from psychiatric harm unless the employer has breached a duty to protect employees from physical harm.

In *Hunter v British Coal Corporation* (1998), Brooke LJ identified three categories of 'primary victim':

- those who fear physical injury to themselves;
- rescuers of the injured;
- those who believe they are or about to be, or have been, the involuntary cause of another's death or injury.

Distinction between primary and secondary victims

Primary victims	Secondary victims
○ No policy control mechanisms to limit the number of claimants.	○ Policy control mechanisms to limit claimants.
○ Foreseeability of physical injury.	○ Foreseeability of injury by way of nervous shock.
○ Issue of foreseeability considered prospectively.	○ Issue of foreseeability considered with hindsight.
○ No distinction between physical or psychiatric injury.	○ Distinction between physical and psychiatric injury.
	○ Foreseeability judged by reference to whether a person of normal fortitude would have suffered a recognisable illness.

Secondary victims

Medically recognised psychiatric illness or disorder
Before there can be liability, in the case of secondary victims,
there must be a medically recognised psychiatric illness or
medical disorder; there is no liability for emotional distress
or grief unless this leads to a recognisable medical condition
these have been held to include:

- depression: *Chadwick v British Transport Commission*
  (1967);

- personality change: *McLoughlin v O'Brian* (1983);

- post traumatic stress disorder: *Hale v London Underground*
  (1992).

It was held in *Hicks v Chief Constable of South Yorkshire* (1992)
that there could be no claim for the terror suffered
immediately before death for the knowledge that death was
imminent.

An abnormally sensitive plaintiff will be unable to recover
unless a person of 'normal' fortitude would have suffered.

The distinction between grief and a recognised psychiatric
condition was again discussed in *Vernon v Bosley (No 1)*
(1996). The plaintiff was found to suffer from Post Traumatic
Stress Disorder (PTSD), complicated by a grief reaction.
While PTSD is recoverable because it is a recognised
psychiatric condition, grief is not compensatable. It was
held by a majority that although the rules of nervous shock
limit the number of potential claimants, they do not limit
the compensation to those who are owed a duty of care.
Even though part of the injury was attributable to grief,
damages were recoverable in full.

Additional criteria

In addition to the above, there are other criteria that the plaintiff will have to satisfy before the plaintiff can recover for nervous shock in the case of secondary victims:

- proximity in terms of relationship – the plaintiff must be in a close and loving relationship with the accident victim. Rescuers are an exception to this rule;

- proximity in terms of time and space – the plaintiff must be at the scene of the accident, in the vicinity of the accident or come across the 'immediate aftermath' of the accident;

- reasonable foreseeability – the plaintiff's injuries must have been reasonably foreseeable;

- there must have been a direct perception of the accident by the plaintiff with the plaintiff's own 'unaided senses'.

Proximity in terms of relationship
Own safety. Initially, the law only allowed recovery where the plaintiff had been put in fear of his own safety: *Dulieu v White* (1901). The plaintiff in *McFarlane v EE Caledonia Ltd* (1994) was a rescuer at the Piper Alpha disaster. It was held that he could not recover even though he was not a person of reasonable fortitude, as he had feared for his own safety.

Fear for the safety of others. Eventually, the law was extended so that recovery was allowed where the plaintiff feared for the safety of others. *Hambrook v Stokes* (1925) is authority for this proposition, although it should be noted that this is a difficult case and evidence was adduced that the plaintiff had feared for her own safety.

Close and loving relationship. In *Alcock v Chief Constable of South Yorkshire* (1992), it was held by the House of Lords that the plaintiff had to be in a 'close and loving relationship' with the accident victim. This approach rejected an earlier approach by the Court of Appeal which tried to put a restriction on the amount of claims by limiting claimants to specific categories, such as parents and spouses.

Nervous shock caused through damage to property. The cases looked at so far have concentrated on nervous shock following the negligent infliction of personal injury on a loved one. Claims have been allowed for damage to property as well as physical injury. The Court of Appeal in *Attia v British Gas* (1988) allowed for nervous shock after the plaintiff witnessed her house burning down as a result of the defendant's negligence in installing central heating.

Rescuers and Employees. Rescuers are an exception to the rule that claimants for nervous shock have to be in a 'close and loving relationship' with the accident victim. In *Chadwick v British Railways Board* (1967), the plaintiff was a passer-by who assisted at the scene of a rail disaster. He did not know the accident victims but was able to recover. In *Hale v London Underground* (1992), a professional rescuer, a fireman, was awarded damages for nervous shock.

Professional rescuers were again allowed to recover in *Frost v Chief Constable of South Yorkshire* (1996). A majority of the Court of Appeal held that rescuers and employees are primary and not secondary victims. This explains the discrepancy between this case and *Alcock*, where victims' relatives did not succeed as they lacked sufficient proximity.

Frost can also be distinguished from *McFarlane v EE Caledonia Ltd*, as, in the latter case, the employee was off duty. He was not owed a duty by his employer, as he was not under an obligation to be at the scene of the Piper Alpha disaster.

An employee is a 'primary victim' when exposed to the risk of physical injury caused by a colleague and is 'directly involved' as a participant in an incident (*Scholfield v Chief Constable of West Yorkshire* (1998)).

The House of Lords held in *White v Chief Constable of South Yorkshire* (1999) that an employer is not under an obligation to protect employees from psychiatric harm unless the employer has breached a duty to protect employees from physical harm. A rescuer who was not himself exposed to physical risk was a secondary victim.

But, rescuers who are employees may be successful in claims for psychiatric injury if the employer fails to provide counselling after the traumatic event. This was suggested in *Leach v Chief Constable of Gloucestershire* (1999) and the argument is being pursued by two policewomen who attended the Dunblane massacre.

Proximity in terms of time and space
Initially, the plaintiff had to be at the scene of the accident to be able to recover for nervous shock. In *Bourhill v Young* (1943), the plaintiff was 50 yards from the scene of the accident which she could hear but could not see and was held to be insufficiently proximate to the scene of the accident. Similarly, in *King v Phillips* (1953), the defendant was a taxi driver who negligently ran over a boy's tricycle. The plaintiff was the boy's mother who witnessed the accident from a distance of 70 yards. It was held that she was insufficiently proximate to the scene of the accident.

However, a change can be detected in the courts' attitude in the case of *Boardman v Sanderson* (1964) where the plaintiff who again heard but was not present at the scene of the accident was able to recover.

In *McLoughlin v O'Brian* (1983), the plaintiff was two miles from the accident but rushed to the hospital to see her family prior to them receiving medical treatment and was held to be sufficiently proximate. She had come across the 'immediate aftermath' of the accident. In *Palmer v Tees Health Authority* (1999), the claim of a mother who saw the body of her murdered child three days after death also failed for lack of proximity.

In *Duncan v British Coal Corporation* (1997), a plaintiff who was 275 metres away from the scene of the accident and arrived at the scene four minutes later but saw no injury or blood was not sufficiently proximate in terms of time and space.

Reasonable foreseeability

In *Bourhill v Young*, the plaintiff did not recover as she was not regarded as being reasonably foreseeable. Two views formed as to the true ratio of the case:

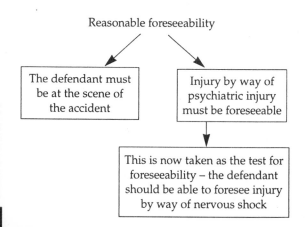

Reasonable foreseeability

The defendant must be at the scene of the accident

Injury by way of psychiatric injury must be foreseeable

This is now taken as the test for foreseeability – the defendant should be able to foresee injury by way of nervous shock

Direct perception

In *McLoughlin v O'Brian*, certain policy issues came to the fore. Lord Wilberforce felt that there was a need to set some limit on the extent of liability and it was therefore necessary to limit claims where there had been a direct perception of the accident with the plaintiff's own unaided senses. Lord Bridge did not see the necessity of setting such an arbitrary limit on claims and did not feel that it was necessary.

For several years after *McLoughlin v O'Brian*, there was considerable uncertainty as to the state of the law. In *Hevican v Ruane* (1991), the plaintiff saw his son's dead body some time after he died, without coming across the 'immediate aftermath' of the accident. Similarly, at first instance, in *Ravenscroft v Rederiaktiebolaget* (1991), the claim of a mother who did not come across the 'immediate aftermath' was initially allowed.

Alcock settled the fact that it had to be a direct perception of the accident with the plaintiff's own unaided senses. *Ravenscroft v Rederiaktiebolaget* was as a result overturned on appeal.

Proposals for reform

The Law Commission in its report, *Liability for Psychiatric Illness*, has recommended reform. It felt that there should be a statutory 'duty of care'. It would leave the rule in *Page v Smith* unaffected but would otherwise require reasonable foreseeability of psychiatric illness as a result of death, injury or imperilment of a person with whom the plaintiff had a close tie of love and affection, regardless of proximity in terms of time and space. Furthermore, the plaintiff would no longer be required to perceive the accident with his own unaided senses.

When proving proximity in terms of love and affection, there would be a fixed set of relationships covered by the statutory duty of care. This would include the following categories of relationship:

- spouse;

- parent;

- child;

- brother or sister (but not step brothers and sisters);

- cohabitees of at least two years standing (including same sex relationships).

Anyone not included on the list would have to prove close ties of love and affection. The statutory duty would not be imposed if it was not 'just and reasonable'.

Economic loss

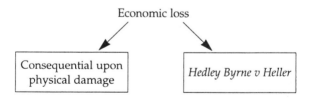

The law of negligence does not give the same level of protection to economic interests as it does to physical interests. There are only three types of situations where recovery is allowed in negligence for economic loss:

- economic loss which is consequential upon physical damage;

- negligent mis-statements;

- 'pockets' of liability which are thought to survive: *Murphy.*

Economic loss which is consequential upon physical damage
It is long established that economic loss as a result of physical injury is recoverable not only for the cost of repairing physical damage to person or property but also for 'consequential' loss of earnings or profits during convalescence or repair.

Much stricter controls apply in relation to 'commercial losses'. Recovery was not allowed in *Weller v Foot and Mouth DRI* even though the damage was foreseeable as damage was also foreseeable to 'countless other enterprises'.

In *Spartan Steel and Alloys v Martin & Co (Contractors) Ltd* (1973), the defendant negligently cut off electricity to the defendant's factory. Damages for the cost of molten metal which was thrown away were recoverable, as it was consequential upon physical damage but loss of profits while electricity was cut off were not recoverable as they were purely commercial profits.

This area was greatly affected by the application of the *Anns* test. In *Junior Books v Veitchi Co Ltd* (1983), recovery was allowed for economic loss in a situation where liability had not been held to exist before. The defendants were subcontractors and flooring specialists and had been nominated by the plaintiffs who had employed the main contractors. The floor was negligently laid and the plaintiffs claimed loss of profits for the period when the law had to be re-laid. Applying the *Anns* test, it was held that the damage was recoverable. This promised to open up a whole new field of claims for economic loss and *Junior Books* has not been followed in subsequent cases, although it has not been formally overruled. The House of Lords found it particularly significant that the sub-contractors had been nominated by the plaintiffs and it was felt that this was sufficient to create a relationship of 'proximity'.

This has become known as the 'high water' mark of economic loss. The courts have since returned to the traditional test. For example, in *Muirhead v Industrial Tank Specialities Ltd* (1986), the plaintiffs who had suffered loss because their lobsters had been killed because of defective motors on a tank could only recover the cost of the lobsters and repairs to the tank, they could not recover for loss of profits. This case has clear echoes of *Spartan Steel*.

This trend was confirmed by the case of *Leigh and Sullivan v Aliakmon Shipping* (1986) which again held that it was not possible to recover economic losses arising from negligent misconduct.

Negligent mis-statements
So far we have looked at liability for negligent acts; the situation is very different when it comes to statements which cause economic loss. One difficulty is that statements may be made on an informal occasion and may be passed on without the consent of the speaker.

Special relationship
The major development in this area came in the case of *Hedley Byrne & Co Ltd v Heller & Partners* (1964) where the House of Lords held that where there was a 'special relationship' between the maker of a statement and the receiver of a statement then there could be liability for the economic loss caused. In this particular case, there was no liability as there had been a disclaimer attached to the

statement, so there had not been a 'voluntary assumption of responsibility'.

The Privy Council in *Mutual Life and Citizens' Assurance Co Ltd v Evatt* (1971) attempted to limit the scope of *Hedley Byrne* by stating that it only applied in respect of advice given in the course of a business and where the defendant made it clear that he was claiming some special skill or competence. (There was, however, a minority view rejecting this approach.)

That attempt has not been followed since and the special relationship has been drawn more liberally. It became clear in *Howard Marine and Dredging Co Ltd v Ogden* (1978) that there had to be *considered* advice which someone would act upon. Liability would not extend to off-the-cuff information.

So, in *Esso Petroleum v Mardon* (1976), the defendants were liable even though they were not in the business of giving advice but they did have experience and special skill and knowledge compared to the plaintiffs.

While, in *Henderson v Merrett Syndicates* Ltd (1994), there was liability for advice given under a contract. In *Holt v Payne Skillington* (1995), it was held that the duty under *Hedley Byrne* could be greater than that in contract.

The Privy Council in *Royal Bank Trust Co Ltd (Trinidad) Ltd v Pampellone* (1987) made a distinction between passing on information and the giving of advice. See, also, *Williams v Natural Life Health Foods* (1998) (HL).

In *Chaudhry v Prabhakar* (1989), liability was imposed when the statement was made on a social occasion but the defendant had specialist knowledge compared to the plaintiff.

Smith v Eric S Bush

Harris v Wyre Forest DC

The plaintiff had applied to a building society for a mortgage and was required to pay for a valuation to be done on the property by the defendants. The valuation contained a disclaimer that the defendants would not be liable in the event of any negligence

↓

Lord Templeman said that the relationship was 'akin to contract' and liability was imposed. In contrast to *Hedley Byrne*, this case was decided after the Unfair Contract Terms Act 1977

↓

The disclaimer failed the reasonableness test The statement had been used for the purpose for which it was intended

Valuation had been carried out by the local authority Valuation had not been shown to the plaintiff and it also contained a disclaimer

↓

Defendants were still found to be liable

Reliance

There must be reliance on the statement by the plaintiff. Take, for example, *Smith v Eric S Bush* (1990) and *Harris v Wyre Forest DC* (1990), two appeals heard together by the House of Lords.

By contrast, a firm of estate agents could rely on a disclaimer in property particulars as against the purchaser of a property in *McCullagh v Lane Fox and Partners Ltd* (1995). The purchaser had not, in that case, been reasonably entitled to believe that the estate agent at the time of making the statement was assuming responsibility for it. The inclusion of a disclaimer put the matter beyond doubt. The Unfair Contract Terms Act 1977 did not preclude the estate agent from relying on the disclaimer.

It was held in *Hemmens v Wilson Browne* (1993) that it could not be reasonable to rely on a statement where a solicitor had advised his client's mistress to obtain independent legal advice before executing a document.

In addition to reliance, there must be knowledge by the maker of the statement, that the recipient will rely on the statement to his detriment. Both requirements were satisfied in *Welton v North Cornwall District Council* (1996). An environmental health officer negligently required the owner of food premises to comply with the Food Act 1990, by making unnecessary substantial building works and major alterations to the kitchen. He also threatened to close the business down, if the works were not completed. The officer knew that what he said would be relied on by the plaintiffs without independent inquiry. He visited to inspect and approved the works. The fact that the relationship arose out of the purported exercise of statutory functions did not give rise to an immunity on the part of the local authority. It was not necessary to consider whether it was fair, just and reasonable to impose a duty, as the case did not involve an incremental extension to the *Hedley Byrne* principle.

Purpose

The courts will take into account the purpose for which the statement was made. In *Caparo Industries plc v Dickman*, the plaintiffs were shareholders in a company and, as such, were entitled to annual audited accounts. On the basis of these accounts, they launched a take-over bid in the company before discovering that the accounts had been negligently audited and had wrongly shown the company to be profit making. The plaintiffs sued the auditors who were found not to be liable. The annual audited accounts were the fulfilment of a statutory obligation the purpose of which was to enable the shareholders to take decisions about the management of the company; it was not intended to be the basis of an investment decision.

There have been other cases concerning annual audited accounts (see the diagram opposite).

Negligent statements relied upon by a third party

An employer who gives a negligent reference about an employee to a prospective employer owes a duty not only to the prospective employer but also to the employee. In *Spring v Guardian Assurance plc* (1994), it was held by the House of Lords that there could be liability in negligence to an employee for an inaccurate reference under the *Hedley Byrne* principle.

This overturned the decision of the Court of Appeal in the same case which held that any right of action would be in defamation where there would be the defence of qualified privilege. This defence would only be defeated by the plaintiff if malice could be proved, which is extremely difficult.

	Al Saudi Banque v Pixley (1989) where auditors did not owe a duty to a bank which had advanced money to a company on the basis of annual audited accounts
Other cases	*Al Nakib Investments* (1990) where accounts were provided to existing shareholders to encourage them to buy additional shares in a rights issue but the plaintiffs used the accounts as the basis of a decision to buy additional shares on the stock market and were consequently held not to be owed a duty
	Mariola Marine Corporation v Lloyd's Register of Shipping (The Morning Watch) (1990) where there was no liability where the survey of a ship had been carried out for the purposes of a health and safety inspection when the results of the survey had been used as the basis of a decision to purchase a ship

Similar situations have arisen where a doctor has examined a plaintiff on behalf of someone else, such as a company. In *Baker v Kaye* (1997), a doctor carried out a pre-employment medical assessment on behalf of a company. It was held that, in such circumstances, a doctor could owe a duty of care to the prospective employee. Although, on the facts of the case, there had been no breach of duty. The case was distinguished from *Spring* as there had never been a contractual relationship between the prospective employer and employee but it was regarded as just and reasonable to impose a duty.

In *Kapfunde v Abbey National plc* (1998), the plaintiff applied for a job and filled in a medical questionnaire. A doctor who considered the questionnaire felt that the plaintiff might be frequently absent from work. The Court of Appeal held that there was no duty of care owed by the doctor to the plaintiff as there was insufficient proximity. The Court of Appeal disapproved of the decision in *Baker v Kaye*.

Concurrent liability
Concurrent liability in contract and tort was allowed in *Henderson v Merrett Syndicates Ltd* (1994).

Voluntary assumption of responsibility other than for negligent mis-statements

There is also a line of cases that allows recovery for pure economic loss in negligence when the special skills of a provider of professional services has been relied on by someone other than his client.

In *Ross v Caunters* (1979), a solicitor allowed the spouse of a beneficiary to witness a will. As a result, the gift to the beneficiary lapsed. It was held that the solicitor was liable to the beneficiary, as damage to her could have been foreseen and she belonged to a closed category of persons.

Ross v Caunters was decided during the period of the *Anns* test. It was uncertain after the demise of that test whether this type of economic loss would remain recoverable. It was found to have survived in the House of Lords decision of *White v Jones* (1995). The testator of a will cut his two daughters out of his estate following a quarrel. After a reconciliation with his daughters, he sent a letter instructing a firm of solicitors that legacies of £9,000 should be given to each of his two daughters, the plaintiffs. The letter was received on 17 July and nothing was done by the solicitors for a month. On 16 August, the firm's managing clerk asked the firm's probate department to draw up a will or codicil incorporating the new legacies. The following day the managing clerk went on holiday and, on his return, a fortnight later he arranged to see the testator on 17 September. The testator died on 14 September before the new will had been executed.

Lord Goff held that the plaintiffs were owed a duty of care as otherwise there would be a lacuna in the law. The solicitor owes a duty of care to his client and generally owes no duty to a third party. If an extension to the *Hedley Byrne* principle were not allowed, there would no method of enforcing the contractual right. Those who had a valid claim (the testator and his estate) had suffered no loss. Those who had suffered a loss (the disappointed beneficiaries) would not have a valid claim. Lord Browne Wilkinson found that the situation was analogous to *Hedley Byrne*.

It was held in *Hemmens v Wilson Browne* (1993) that the principle would not extend to an *inter vivos* transaction, as it would always be possible to rectify a mistake.

White v Jones could not be relied on in *Goodwill v British Pregnancy Advisory Service* (1996). A woman who knew that her partner had undergone a vasectomy did not use any form of contraception and subsequently became pregnant. Her partner had been assured by the defendants that the operation had been successful and that future contraception was unnecessary. It was argued that the situation was analogous to *White v Jones*. The plaintiff was not owed a duty as it was not known that the advice would be communicated to the advisee and would be acted upon by her. She belonged to an indeterminate class of women with whom the man could have formed a relationship after the operation.

Some indication of the scope of the duty is provided by *Woodward v Wolferstans* (1997). The plaintiff had purchased a property raising 95% of the purchase price by way of mortgage. The defendants were a firm of solicitors who acted for her father who guaranteed the mortgage. There was no contact between the firm and the plaintiff. After the mortgage fell into arrears, the lender commenced possession proceedings. It was held that the defendants had assumed responsibility for tasks which were known or ought to be known to closely affect the plaintiff's economic well being. This did not extend to explaining the details of the transaction and the implications of the mortgage.

Exercise of statutory powers

This area deals with the question whether public authorities exercising statutory powers owe any duty to a private individual suffering loss or injury resulting from the authority's negligence.

There are three problems in this area:

- many statutory powers confer a discretion as to how and whether the relevant power should be exercised;

- where the alleged negligence is a failure to exercise statutory power, the question of liability for omissions is raised in its most obvious form;

- recent case law requires the individual to pursue a remedy in the form of judicial review as opposed to tort.

The problem of whether a duty of care will ever be imposed in respect of the negligent exercise of statutory powers and the problem of liability for failure to exercise a power can now be considered together.

In *Home Office v Dorset Yacht Co Ltd*, the Home Office had a wide discretion as to how to run its Borstal Training Schools. If the Home Office owed a duty to individuals for damage caused by escaping trainees, then it might be inhibited in the exercise of its discretion. Lord Diplock stipulated that the Home Office would only be liable for *ultra vires* acts of its servants. The Borstal Officers had disregarded an order and so their conduct was *ultra vires*. The duty was only owed to those in the immediate vicinity whose property was reasonably foreseeably likely to be damaged or stolen in the immediate escape of inmates.

His reasoning was further developed in *Anns v Merton LBC* where the local authority argued that it had merely exercised a power and had not been under a mandatory duty to inspect all foundations. The authority argued that:

- it would not be liable for omitting to inspect; and
- if it was not liable for inspecting, it could not be liable for negligent inspection.

Again, it was stated that *ultra vires* conduct could create a duty of care, and that *ultra vires* conduct could be a failure to exercise a power at all, or an improper exercise of that power.

The House of Lords made a distinction between:

- planning/policy decisions; and
- operational decisions,

and stated that they would be far more likely to find a duty of care where there had been an operational error and would be less likely to interfere with policy matters.

Although *Anns* was overruled by *Murphy v Brentwood DC*, the policy/operational dichotomy is still valid. It was said in *Rowling v Takaro* (1988) that there was no automatic liability for operational decisions but the distinction could be seen as a preliminary filter. Policy decisions would be automatically filtered out, but once this step had been overcome, then there is a need to decide whether a duty should be imposed on the basis of foreseeability, proximity and whether it is fair, just and reasonable to do so.

There has been a trend of restricting the tort of negligence in this area. In *Yuen Kun-Yeu v AG of Hong Kong* (1987), *Rowling v Takaro Properties* (1988) and *Davis v Radcliffe* (1990), the factors that were cited as militating against a duty of care were similar, for example, the distorting effect of potential liability on the decision making process; the waste of public money involved in civil servants cautiously investigating the case to the detriment of other members of the public; the difficulty of ever proving negligence in the making of such a decision; and the difficulty of distinguishing the cases in which legal advice should have been sought.

This generally restrictive approach to negligence claims in this area appears to be a reluctance to introduce the tortious duty of care where there is an existing system of redress or the statutory regulatory system has made no provision for individual claims.

This trend towards the containment of negligence actions can be seen in *Jones v Department of Employment* (1988) where one of the grounds of the Court of Appeal's decision that a social security adjudication officer owed no duty of care to a claimant was that the duty of the adjudication officer lay in the sphere of public law and was only enforceable by way of statutory appeals procedure or by judicial review.

The House of Lords again held that policy decisions were outside the scope of negligence in *X v Bedfordshire County Council* (1995). It was held that where a statutory discretion was imposed on a local authority, it was for the authority to exercise the discretion and nothing which the authority would do within the ambit of the discretion could be actionable at common law.

Where the decision complained of fell outside the statutory discretion, it could give rise to common law liability but where the factors relevant to the exercise of the discretion included matters of policy, the court could not adjudicate on such policy matters and therefore could not reach the decision that it was outside the statutory ambit.

The same conclusion was reached in *Stovin v Wise* (1996). A highway authority was held not to be liable in negligence for failing to remove a hazard to the highway under statutory powers conferred by the Highway Act 1980, even though the authority was aware of the danger and had decided that it ought to remove the hazard but had failed to do so.

Lord Hoffman said that the minimum pre-conditions for basing a duty of care on the existence of a statutory power were first, it would have to have been irrational not to have exercised the power, so that there was a public duty to act and secondly, there were exceptional grounds for holding that the policy of the statute required compensation to be paid to persons who suffered loss because the power was not exercised.

Another reason advanced for not imposing a duty on public authorities is that it would lead to defensiveness in their decision making. In *Harris v Evans* (1998), a Health and Safety inspector making negligently excessive requirements of bungee jump operators when making recommendations as to whether activities should be authorised under the Health and Safety at Work Act 1974 was not liable. It was part of the system of regulation that it would have adverse impacts for certain sections of society. There was an appeals mechanism built into the legislation and a common law duty of care would lead to inspectors being defensive in the exercise of their enforcement powers under the Act.

A duty will also not be imposed on a public authority if it would not be fair, just or reasonable or a common law duty would be inconsistent with or discourage, the due performance by the public authority of its statutory duties. In *Clunis v Camden and Islington Health Authority* (1998), the plaintiff had been detained under the Mental Health Act 1983. Following his discharge, the defendants under s 117 of the same Act were under a duty to provide after care services but failed to do so. Three months after discharge, he killed a stranger and was convicted of manslaughter. He was ordered to be detained in a special hospital. It was held not to be fair or reasonable to hold the defendant liable for the plaintiff's criminal act.

Public authorities will be held liable where they are not exercising a statutory function. In *W v Essex County Council* (1998), a local authority placed a known 15 year old sex abuser with a family with no warning. The result was that the children of the family were abused by the foster child. The parents had inquired about the child's history and had wrongly been given assurances that there was no history of sex abuse. The local authority were not exercising a statutory function with respect to the children of the family and owed them a duty of care.

The assurances given by the local authority constituted a voluntary assumption of responsibility and gave rise to a duty of care under *Hedley Byrne* principles.

Breach of duty: standard of care

Having established that the defendant owes the plaintiff a duty of care, it will next be necessary to determine whether the defendant has in fact breached that duty. The defendant will have fulfilled his duty if he has behaved in accordance with the standard of the reasonable man. This is an objective standard and disregards the personal idiosyncrasies of the defendant. Everyone is judged by the same standard, the only exceptions being skilled defendants, children and the insane and physically ill.

The question whether a person has fulfilled a particular duty is a question of FACT. It was ' y the House of Lords in *Qualcast (Wolverhampton) Ltd ⌐aynes* (1959) that reasonableness will depend on the circumstances of the case and it is a mistake to rely on previous cases as precedents for what constitutes negligence. So, in *Worsfold v Howe* (1980), the trial judge held that a driver who had edged out from a side road and across stationary tankers before colliding with a motor-cyclist was negligent as the Court of Appeal had ruled that similar actions were negligent in a previous case. The Court of Appeal held that the previous case laid down no legal principle, that such decisions were to be treated as questions of fact.

Factors of the objective standard
The law provides various guiding principles as to the objective standard.

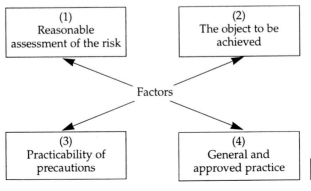

(1) Reasonable assessment of the risk

This can be further subdivided into two factors:

- degree of likelihood of harm occurring;
- seriousness of the harm that may occur.

Bolton v Stone (1951)	*Miller v Jackson* (1977)
A cricket ball had been hit out of a cricket ground six times in 28 years into a nearby, rarely used lane. On the seventh occasion, it hit a passer-by in the lane	A cricket ball was hit out of a ground eight to nine times a season

Held: the chances of such an accident occurring were so small that it was not reasonable to expect the defendant to take precautions against it happening	*Held:* the defendant had been negligent as it was reasonable to expect the defendant to take precautions

(a) *Degree of likelihood of harm occurring.* A reasonable man is not usually expected to take precautions against something where there is only a small risk of it occurring. Two cricketing cases provide a simple illustration:

Difference: the crucial difference between the two cases is that the risk of harm was much greater in *Miller v Jackson* than in *Bolton v Stone*.

(b) *Seriousness of the harm that may occur*. This is an exception to the above, that is, where there is a small risk but the potential harm that may occur is great then a reasonable man would be expected to take precautions.

Paris v Stepney BC (1951)

The plaintiff was blind in one eye. While he was working for the defendants, a metal chip entered his good eye and rendered him totally blind. The defendants were found to be negligent in failing to supply him with goggles as even though there had only been a small risk, the consequences were serious

---

(2) The object to be achieved

The importance of the object to be attained is also a factor which is taken into account when deciding the standard of care. It is necessary to assess the utility of the defendant's act. The greater its social utility, the greater the likelihood of the defendant's behaviour being assessed as reasonable.

Watt v Hertfordshire CC (1954)

The plaintiff was a fireman and part of a rescue team that was rushing to the scene of an accident to rescue a woman trapped under a car. The plaintiff was injured by a heavy piece of equipment which had not been properly secured on the lorry on which it was travelling in the emergency circumstances. It was held that it was necessary to 'balance the risk against the object to be achieved'. The action for negligence failed as the risk of the equipment causing injury in transit was not so great as to prevent the efforts to save the woman's life

> *Latimer v AEC Ltd* (1953)
>
> The defendant's factory was flooded, the water mixed with factory oil and made the floor slippery. Sawdust was spread on the surface but not enough to cover the whole affected area

(3) Practicability of precautions

The cost of avoiding a risk is also a material factor in the standard of care. The defendant will not be expected to spend vast sums of money on avoiding a risk which is very small.

It was held that the employers were not negligent. It was necessary to balance the risk against the measures necessary to eliminate it. In this case the risk was not so great as to justify the expense of closing the factory down.

(4) General and approved practice

If it is shown that the defendant acted in accordance with general and approved practice, then this may be strong evidence that he has not been negligent. However, this is not conclusive and a defendant may still be negligent even though he acted in accordance with a common practice.

There is a obligation on the defendant to keep up to date with developments and to change practices in the light of new knowledge: *Stokes v Guest, Keen and Nettleford (Bolts and Nuts) Ltd* (1968).

It will not be a defence to say that general and approved practice has been followed if it is an obvious folly to do so. 'Neglect of duty does not by repetition cease to be neglect of duty', *per* Slesser LJ, *Carpenters' Co v British Mutual Banking Co Ltd* (1937).

The doctrine of 'obvious folly' was first expounded by Lord Dunedin in *Morton v William Dixon Ltd* (1907) and a recent illustration can be found in *Re the Herald of Free Enterprise* (1987). Following the Zeebrugge ferry disaster, the master of the ship claimed that it was general and approved practice for him not to check that the bow doors were closed prior to setting out to sea. It was held that the general and approved practice constituted an 'obvious folly' and should not have been followed.

Failure to comply with a guide to professional conduct is not conclusive proof of negligence (*Johnson v Bingley* (1995)).

The general standard and skilled defendants
Skilled defendants are judged by higher standards than the ordinary defendant. The test for skilled defendants was encapsulated by McNair J in *Bolam v Friern Hospital Management Committee* (1957):

> The test is the standard of the ordinary skilled man exercising and professing to have that particular skill. A man need not possess the highest expert skill at the risk of being found negligent. It is well established law that it is sufficient if he exercises the ordinary skill of an ordinary competent man exercising that particular art.

It can be seen that skilled defendants must meet a higher standard than the ordinary person and this is an exception to the rule that everyone is judged by the same standard.

Skilled defendants face a particular problem when trying to invoke the defence of general and approved practice, as often there are conflicting views within a profession as to which course of action is the appropriate course to take. *Bolam* gave an answer to this problem as it stated that a doctor was not negligent if he acted in accordance with a respectable body of opinion merely because another body of opinion took a contrary view. It was also held that a doctor could not be criticised if he believed dangers of treatment were minimal and did not stress them to the patient.

Bolam was applied in the case of *Sidaway v Bethlem Royal Hospital Govrs* (1985), where it was held that a doctor was under a duty to inform a patient of special/real risks but this is subject to an overriding duty to act in the patient's best interest.

However, conditions were attached to the *Bolam* test in *Bolitho v City and Hackney Health Authority* (1997). A two year old boy suffered brain damage as a result of the bronchial air passages becoming blocked leading to cardiac arrest. It was agreed that the only course of action to prevent the damage was to have the boy intubated. The doctor who negligently failed to attend the boy said that she would not have intubated had she attended. There was evidence from one expert witness that he would not have intubated, whereas five other experts said that they would have done so.

The House of Lords held that there would have to be a logical basis for the opinion not to intubate. This would involve a weighing of risks against benefit in order to achieve a defensible conclusion. In effect, this means that a judge will be entitled to choose between two bodies of expert opinion and to reject an opinion which is 'logically indefensible'.

Trainee experts

The potential harshness of the objective standard for skilled defendants is illustrated by the case of *Wilsher v Essex Area Health Authority* (1988) when it was stated that a young, inexperienced doctor is judged by the standards of a competent experienced doctor even though, by definition, he is unable to attain that standard.

Experts outside the medical field

The same principles extend outside the medical sphere. In *Wells v Cooper* (1958), the Court of Appeal held that a householder performing a DIY task was judged by the standard of a reasonably competent carpenter.

In *Phillips v William Whiteley* (1938), the court rejected the idea that a jeweller who carried out an ear piercing operation should be judged by the standard of a surgeon but instead the court said that she should be judged by the standard of a reasonably competent jeweller carrying out that particular task.

In *Nettleship v Weston* (1971), a learner driver was judged by the standard of a 'competent and experienced driver' as she held herself out as possessing a certain standard of skill and experience. The court felt that a uniform standard of skill was preferable because of the practical difficulty of assessing a particular person's actual skill or experience.

Expert standard depends on the surrounding circumstances

In the same way as the ordinary standard, the expert standard depends on the circumstances of the particular case.

In *Wooldridge v Sumner* (1963), a momentary lapse on the part of a showjumper did not make him negligent.

Wooldridge v Sumner involved a participant in a sporting event injuring a spectator. In *Smolden v Whitworth* (1996), the court held that a rugby referee's level of care to a participant in a sporting event was that appropriate in all the circumstances. The threshold of liability was a high one and would not be easily crossed. On the facts of the case, the referee was liable for spinal injuries caused by a collapsed scrum.

Abnormal defendants

Further exceptions to the rule that everyone is judged by the same standard in assessing whether they are negligent are children and the insane and the physically ill. Both categories are treated separately and different principles apply.

(1) Children

In *Gough v Thorne* (1966), Lord Denning said that a 12 year old child could not be contributorily negligent. In *Walmsley v Humewick* (1954), it was held that very young children were incapable of negligence as they were incapable of foreseeing harm. It should be noted that in tort there is no fixed age for liability unlike in criminal law.

A problem with children has been in deciding whether subjective circumstances such as the child's mental ability and maturity be taken into account or should an objective standard be applied in the same way as for adults?

The High Court of Australia in *McHale v Watson* (1966) held that a 12 year old boy should be judged by 'the foresight and prudence of an ordinary boy of 12'.

McHale v Watson was followed by the Court of Appeal in *Mullin v Richards* (1998). Two 15 year olds were playing with plastic rulers when one broke and a piece of plastic entered the plaintiff's eye. The test was whether the risk of injury would have been foreseeable to an ordinarily prudent and reasonable 15 year old girl.

(2) The insane and the physically ill

The principles which apply here seem to revolve around whether the defendant was aware of his condition and also whether the defendant had control over his own actions.

- *Defendant is unaware of the condition*

  In *Waugh v Allan* (1964), the defendant, a lorry driver, was in the habit of suffering gastric attacks which normally quickly passed. After one such attack, the defendant pulled off the road and, when he felt better, continued on his journey only to suffer a fatal coronary thrombosis and injured the plaintiff. The defendant was held not to be negligent as he had recovered sufficient skill and judgment to continue his journey.

  In *Jones v Dennison* (1971), the defendant was unaware that he suffered from blackout attacks as a result of epilepsy. He suffered a blackout while driving, injuring the plaintiff. It was held that he could not be considered negligent, as he was unaware of his tendency to blackout.

- *Defendant retains control over his actions*

  In situations where the defendant retains some control over his actions, he will be held liable.

  In *Roberts v Ramsbottom* (1980), the defendant suffered a stroke shortly after starting a two and a half mile journey. He had two collisions before colliding with the plaintiff's parked vehicle. It was found that he was aware of the collisions and had retained some impaired control over his actions and consequently was liable.

  In *Morris v Marsden* (1952), the defendant suffered from a mental disease which robbed him of his moral judgment. While suffering from this disease, he attacked and injured the plaintiff; while he knew the nature and quality of his act, he did not know that what he was doing was wrong. The defendant was held to be liable.

Proof of breach
The burden of proof rests with the plaintiff on the balance of probabilities.

However, there may be ways in which the plaintiff can receive assistance in discharging that burden of proof.

(1) Assistance by statute
Section 11 of the Civil Evidence Act 1968. Where the defendant has been convicted of criminal proceedings, that conviction will be admissible in civil proceedings and the defendant will be taken to have committed the acts until the contrary is proved.

For example, proof of the defendant's conviction for careless driving places the burden of disproving the occurrence of negligent driving on the defendant.

(2) Assistance at common law
Res ipsa loquitur. 'The thing speaks for itself.' This doctrine originally began with the case of *Scott v London and St Katherine's Dock* (1865). First, it should be noted that it is an evidential burden and, secondly, three conditions must apply before it can be invoked:

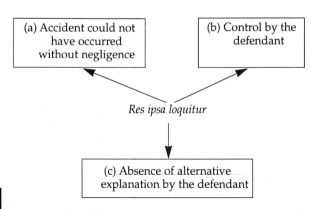

```
(a) Accident could not          (b) Control by the
    have occurred                   defendant
    without negligence

                  Res ipsa loquitur

            (c) Absence of alternative
            explanation by the defendant
```

(a) Accident could not have occurred without negligence

For example, stones are not found in buns unless someone has been negligent: *Chaproninière v Mason* (1905); barrels of flour do not fall from warehouse windows onto the street in the absence of negligence: *Byrne v Boadle* (1863). On the other hand, losses on the commodity market are not *prima facie* evidence of negligence on the part of brokers: *Stafford v Conti Commodity Services Ltd* (1981); nor is a spark from a domestic fire: *Sochaki v Sas* (1947).

In *Scott v London and St Katherine's Docks Co*, it was said that the accident must have happened in 'the ordinary course of things'. As a result, the issue has arisen whether the doctrine can apply to matters which are outside the common experience. In *Mahon v Osborne* (1939), a swab had been left inside a patient after an abdominal operation; Scott LJ thought that the doctrine could not apply to surgical operations as they are outside a judge's common experience. Since then, the Court of Appeal have allowed the doctrine to be invoked in cases of medical negligence in *Cassidy v Ministry of Health* (1951). Although it was said by Lord Denning in *Hucks v Cole* (1968) that *res ipsa loquitur* could only be invoked against a doctor in 'extreme' cases. This adds to the plaintiff's difficulties in cases of medical negligence which statistically are harder to prove than other types of negligence.

(b) Control by the defendant

If the defendant is not in control of the situation which could not have occurred without negligence, then the doctrine cannot be invoked.

In *Eason v London and North Eastern Railway Co* (1944), the railway company could not be said to be in control of railway doors on a journey Edinburgh to London, because of the possibility of interference by a third party.

This can be contrasted with *Gee v Metropolitan Railway Co* (1873) where someone fell trough a train door shortly after it left the station. Here, it could be said to be under the control of the railway company, as there was no opportunity for third party interference.

(c) Absence of alternative explanation by the defendant

The cause of the accident must be unknown: *Barkway v South Western Transport* (1950).

The effect of the doctrine of res ipsa loquitur

The effect of *res ipsa loquitur* depends principally on the cogency of the inference. The more cogent the inference the greater the defendant's task in overcoming assumptions of negligence. The effect, therefore, is subjective and depends on the case but two views have been formed as to the effect:

- *An evidential burden of proof is cast on the defendant*
  In other words, the defendant is required to provide a reasonable explanation of how the accident could have occurred without negligence on his part. If he does so, then the plaintiff goes back to square one and must prove on the balance of probabilities that the defendant has been negligent. Support for this view can be found in *Colvilles Ltd v Devine* (1969).

- *The other view is that it reverses the burden of proof*
  The defendant must prove on the balance of probabilities, that he has not been negligent. Support for this view can be found in *Henderson v Jenkins* (1970) and *Ward v Tesco Stores* (1976). The Privy Council in *Ng Chun Pui v Lee Chuen Tat* (1988) stated that the burden of proof does not shift to the defendant but remains with the

plaintiff throughout the case. It has also been argued that if *res ipsa loquitur* reverses the burden of proof then paradoxically a plaintiff who relies on the maxim will be in a better position than a plaintiff who establishes a *prima facie* case in some other way.

Causation

The plaintiff not only has to prove that the defendant owes him a duty of care and has breached his duty but also that the defendant caused the plaintiff's loss. This is not always as obvious as it sounds.

'But for' test

The defendant's breach of duty must as a matter of fact be a cause of the damage. As a preliminary test in deciding whether the defendant's breach has caused the plaintiff's damage, the courts have developed the 'but for' test. In other words, would the plaintiff not have suffered the damage 'but for' the event brought about by the defendant?

An example of the working of the test is contained in *Barnett v Chelsea and Kensington Hospital Management Committee* (1969). Three nightwatchmen called into a hospital at the end of a shift, complaining that they had been vomiting after drinking tea. The nurse on duty consulted a doctor by telephone and he said that the men should go home and consult their doctor in the morning. Later the same day, the plaintiff's husband died of arsenic poisoning.

The doctor owed the plaintiff's husband a duty of care. In failing to examine the plaintiff's husband the doctor had breached his duty of care but the hospital were held not to be liable as the breach had not caused the death. The plaintiff's husband would have died even if the doctor had examined him. Applying the 'but for' test, would the plaintiff not have suffered the damage 'but for' the event brought about by the defendant? The answer has to be no.

Further examples of the 'but for' test can be found in *Robinson v Post Office* (1974) where a doctor was held not to be liable for failing to administer a test dose of a drug where it would have failed to have revealed the allergy; *McWilliams v Sir William Arrol and Co Ltd* (1962) where employers were found not to be liable for failing to provide a safety belt where it was proved that the employee would not have worn it even if it had been provided; and *The Empire Jamaica* (1957) where liability was limited to 'actual fault' and the only fault that could be attributed to the owners was a failure to apply for a mate's certificate which would have been granted as a formality.

Nature of the 'but for' test

It is vital to keep the following points in mind:

* it acts as a preliminary filter, that is, it sifts irrelevant causes from relevant causes;

* it has no application where there are several successive causes of an accident.

Several successive causes

The 'but for' test will not be of much assistance where the plaintiff has been affected by two successive acts or events. In this type of situation there has been a sequence of events and every act in the sequence is a relevant cause as far as the plaintiff's damage is concerned so the courts have to decide the operative cause.

The courts have not always been consistent in their approach. One method is to establish whether the later event has added to the plaintiff's damage, if not then the person who caused the original injury will be liable.

In *Performance Cars Ltd v Abraham* (1962), the plaintiff's Rolls Royce had been involved in an accident and the damage involved the cost of respraying the car. Two weeks later the defendant was involved in an accident with the plaintiff for which the defendant accepted responsibility. This time, there was damage to the wing and bumper which necessitated a respray of the lower part of the car. The defendant was not liable as he had not contributed any more damage than had occurred after the first accident.

A similar sequence took place in *Baker v Willoughby* (1970). As a result of the defendant's negligence, the plaintiff suffered an injury to his left leg. Before the trial and while working at a new job the plaintiff was the victim of an armed robbery and suffered gunshot wounds to his left leg which then had to be amputated. The defendants argued that their liability was extinguished by the second incident. In other words, they were only liable from the date of the accident to the date of the bank robbery. The House of Lords rejected this. They held that the plaintiff was being compensated for his loss of amenity, that is, the loss of a good left leg, the difference between a damaged leg and a sound leg. The fact that the leg was further damaged at some later date did not alter the fact that he had already been deprived of a perfectly good left leg.

In both these cases, there have been two successive incidents and the second incident has not added to the plaintiff's loss so the perpetrator of the first incident has remained liable. This can be contrasted with *Jobling v Associated Dairies Ltd* (1982). The facts were that the defendants negligently caused an injury to the plaintiff's back. Three years later and

TORT LAW

before trial, the plaintiff was diagnosed as suffering from a condition called mylopathy which was unrelated to the accident. This time, it was accepted, in contrast to the other cases, the second incident extinguished liability. The main differences between these cases have been identified as follows:

- in *Jobling*, the second incident occurred as a result of a natural condition, whereas in *Baker v Willoughby* there was an intervention by a third party;

- policy decisions on the part of the court. If the court had accepted that the second incident extinguished liability in *Baker*, this would have left the defendant without compensation after the second incident.

Simultaneous events

The pragmatic approach of the courts was again evident in the case of *Fitzgerald v Lane* (1987). The facts were that the plaintiff crossed a pelican crossing when the red light was showing, he was hit by the first defendant's car and thrown onto the car's windscreen, then onto the ground and while lying on the ground the second defendant ran over him. It was impossible to determine each defendant's contribution towards the injury. He could have suffered slight injuries from the first defendant and been badly injured by the second or *vice versa*. The court held that after taking into account the plaintiff's contributory negligence, both defendants were equally liable.

Similarly, in *Jenkins v Holt* (1999), it was held that, where two drivers collided, and each could have avoided injury, if they had seen the other, they were both equally liable. Bad driving by one did not make him entirely responsible, if each could have avoided a collision.

Multiple causes

So far, we have looked at situations where there have been a sequence of events. Slightly different issues arise when there are several possible causes of an injury. Again, the courts' approach has not always been consistent.

(1) Where breach of duty materially increases the risk of injury, the defendant will be held liable

In *McGhee v National Coal Board* (1972), the defendants failed to supply adequate washing facilities. Although this could not be proved to have caused the defendant's dermatitis there was evidence to suggest that it had increased the risk of contracting the disease. This was sufficient to make the defendant liable.

(2) The more recent trend is to state that for the defendant to be liable the defendant's cause must be the probable cause

In *Wilsher v Essex Area Health Authority* (1988), the plaintiff's injury could have been caused by one of six possible causes. One of these causes was the administration of an excess of oxygen in the first 30 hours of the baby's birth, which had been carried out by the doctor. It was held that the plaintiff had to prove that the excess of oxygen was the probable cause of the injury, not that it had increased the baby's risk of being born blind.

This approach was followed in *Hotson v East Berkshire Area Health Authority* (1987). The facts were that a boy fell out of a tree injuring his hip. He was rushed to hospital but the injury wasn't diagnosed for five days. The boy developed a hip condition. There was a 75% chance that the condition would have developed anyway and a 25%

chance that the delay in diagnosis had caused the condition. The trial judge reduced damages by 75%. On appeal, it was held that this approach was incorrect. The defendants would not be liable unless their cause was the probable cause. As it was more likely that the condition would have developed anyway, then the most probable cause was that it had developed as a result of the fall. The defendants were not liable.

The approach in *Wilshier* and *Hotson* in deciding causation questions has not been followed in other areas of negligence outside of personal injury. In the negligent mis-statement case of *First Interstate Bank of California v Cohen Arnold & Co* (1995), damages were awarded on a basis that was proportionate to the likelihood of the event occurring. The defendants were a firm of accountants and in a letter grossly overestimated the worth of their client to the plaintiffs, a bank. As a result of the letter, the plaintiffs delayed enforcing their security. The property was sold for £1.4 million. If it had been sold when the bank first made inquiries as to the client's worth, it would have been worth £3 million. There was a 66% chance that they would have sold when they first made inquiries, so damages were reduced to £2 million.

Omissions

If the negligent conduct takes the form of an omission, special difficulties arise. The court must consider what would have happened if the defendant had acted instead of omitting to do so. The issue will then be whether the omission to act made any difference to the outcome. In cases involving special skills, the *Bolam* test, as modified by *Bolitho,* will then apply (*Bolitho v City and Hackney Health Authority* (1997)).

Intervening acts that break the chain of causation:
novus actus interveniens

Sometimes, something can occur between the defendant's act and the plaintiff's injury, which breaks the chain of causation so the defendant can no longer be said to be liable to the plaintiff. This is a *novus actus interveniens*.

It was described by Lord Wright in the *The Oropesa* (1943):

> … a new cause which disturbs the sequence of events, something which can be described as either unreasonable or extraneous or extrinsic.

The facts of *The Oropesa* (1943) were that two ships collided. The captain of one ship put out to sea in heavy weather in a lifeboat to discuss the situation with the captain of the other ship and was drowned. It was argued that this constituted a *novus actus* but this was rejected as it was held that the decision to put out to sea was reasonable in the circumstances.

A rescuer's intervention will not be considered a *novus actus*, as long as the peril is active: *Haynes v Harwood* (1935).

The courts have been quite lenient in what they consider to be a reasonable act. In *Philco Radio and Television Corporation of Great Britain Ltd v J Spurling and Others* (1949), it was held that the act of a typist in touching film scrap with a lighted cigarette with the intention of causing a 'small innocuous fire' but with the result that she caused a serious fire and explosion when the scrap had been wrongly delivered to the plaintiff's premises was not a *novus actus* as it was not an unreasonable act in the circumstances, even though it was unforeseeable.

For an intervening act to constitute a *novus actus*, it must be something in the order of an illegal act such as in *Knightley v Johns* (1982) where a police officer, contrary to police standing orders, sent a police motor-cyclist the wrong way through a tunnel without first sealing the tunnel off. This constituted a *novus actus*.

However, not every illegal act constitutes a *novus actus*, as in *Rouse v Squires* (1973) where the court required a reckless, negligent act. The first defendant caused a motorway accident; a second driver who was driving too fast and failed to keep a proper look out collided with the stationary vehicles. The first driver was held partially to be responsible for the additional damage as the intervening conduct had not been so reckless as to constitute a *novus actus*. This approach was followed in *Wright v Lodge* (1993) where the first defendant negligently left her car on the carriageway in thick fog. The second defendant was deemed to be driving recklessly when he collided with the first defendant's car when driving at 60 mph before swerving across the carriageway and crashing into several cars. It was held that the second driver's recklessness broke the chain of causation and the first defendant could not be held liable for the damage suffered by the other drivers.

Knightley v Johns is hard to reconcile with *Rouse v Squires* and *Wright v Lodge* and the differences arise as a result of policy decisions on the part of the court. In the words of Stephenson LJ in *Knightley v Johns,* the court looks at 'common sense rather than logic on the facts and circumstances of each case'.

Acts of the plaintiff

The plaintiff's acts can constitute a *novus actus*, as in *McKew v Holland and Hannen and Cubitts* (1969) where the defendants had injured the plaintiff's left leg. One day, as the plaintiff was descending some stairs he felt that his leg was about to give way so he jumped down the remaining stairs, thereby injuring his right leg. The plaintiff's act constituted a *novus actus* as it had been an unreasonable act in the circumstances.

By contrast, in *Wieland v Cyril Lord Carpets* (1969), the plaintiff's neck had been injured by the defendants and as a consequence she was required to wear a surgical collar. She fell as she had been unable to use her bifocal spectacles with her usual skill and suffered further injuries. The additional injuries were held to be attributable to the defendant's original negligence.

In *Kirkham v Chief Constable of Greater Manchester* (1990), it was held that the suicide of a prisoner in police custody was not a *novus actus*. The police were under a duty to guard the prisoner to prevent that type of incident occurring.

The reasoning was followed in *Reeves v Commissioner of Police of the Metropolis* (1998). This case also concerned a prisoner who committed suicide in police custody. It was not a *novus actus* as, in the words of Lord Bingham CJ, it was '... the very thing against which the defendant was duty bound to take precautions'.

Morritt LJ in a dissenting judgment said that the duty would only apply where the prisoner was of unsound mind and would not apply to a sane prisoner.

Remoteness of damage

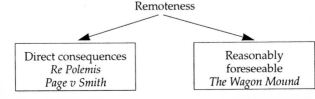

Theoretically, the consequences of conduct are endless; so, even where the defendant has breached a duty, there must be some 'cut off' point beyond which the defendant will not be liable. If a defendant was responsible for his actions *ad infinitum* human activity would be unreasonably hampered.

Since 1850, there have been two competing views as the test for remoteness of damage:

(1) Consequences are too remote if a reasonable man would not have foreseen them: *The Wagon Mound* (1967).

(2) The defendant is liable for all the direct consequences of his act suffered by the plaintiff, whether a reasonable man would have foreseen them or not, no matter how unusual or unexpected: *Re Polemis and Furness, Withy & Co Ltd* (1921).

The Wagon Mound lays down the rule that foreseeability of damage is the test not only for the imposition of a duty of care but also for remoteness of damage. Remember in this context we are looking at liability for the extent of damage, not whether a duty exists.

Manner of occurrence of damage need not be foreseeable
If the type of injury is foreseeable, then the manner in which it occurs need not be foreseeable: *Hughes v Lord Advocate* (1963) but note that this case was distinguished in *Doughty v Turner Manufacturing Co Ltd* (1964).

Type of injury must be foreseeable
In *Tremain v Pike* (1969), the plaintiff was a herdsman who was employed by the defendants and he contracted Weil's Disease, which is an extremely rare disease, is caught by coming into contact with rats' urine. It was held that injury through food contamination was foreseeable, a 'rare

disease' was a different type of injury and was not therefore foreseeable.

However, the House of Lords in *Page v Smith* (1995) awarded damages for psychiatric injury, even though only physical injury was foreseeable. It was held that, in the case of primary victims, there should be no distinction between physical and psychiatric injury.

Again it was said by the Court of Appeal *obiter* in *Giblett v P and NE Murray Ltd* (1999) that, where physical injury is foreseeable in an accident, damages for consequent psychiatric injury were recoverable in principle. Foreseeability of psychological harm need not be shown. On the facts of the case, no causal link was established.

The extent of the damage need not be foreseeable: thin skull rule

Provided the *type* of injury is foreseeable, the defendant will be liable for its full extent even if that is greater than could have been foreseen, due to some peculiar susceptibility, for example, thin skull. This is some residuary hangover from the days of *Re Polemis*.

So, in *Bradford v Robinson Rentals* (1967), a lorry driver was subject to extreme cold and suffered frost-bite as a result. The defendants were liable for the frost-bite even though this was greater than could have been foreseen because the type of injury was foreseeable. This can be contrasted with *Tremain v Pike*, where the type of injury had not been foreseeable.

Impecuniosity of the plaintiff

There is a duty in tort to mitigate one's loss, that is, not increase one's loss unnecessarily. Problems arise where the defendant is too impecunious to be able to afford to mitigate his loss. The courts have not always been consistent in their approach. In *Liesbosch Dredger v SS Edison* (1933), the plaintiff's had been put to much greater expense in fulfilling a contract because they were too poor to buy a substitute dredger for the one which had been damaged by the defendants. It was held that the plaintiff's impecuniosity had to be disregarded and they were unable to recover the additional expenses.

This can be contrasted with more recent cases, such as *Dodd Properties Ltd v Canterbury City Council* (1980) and *Martindale v Duncan* where delays in repair caused by impecuniosity and the cost of substitute hire vehicles were allowed. It was said in *Mattocks v Mann* (1993) that *The Liesbosch* was constantly being reviewed in the light of changed circumstances and hire charges were again allowed.

2 Occupiers' liability

Liability under the Occupiers' Liability Act 1957

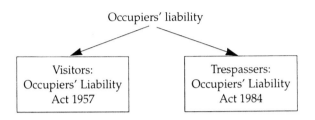

Occupiers' liability

Visitors:
Occupiers' Liability
Act 1957

Trespassers:
Occupiers' Liability
Act 1984

Who is an 'occupier' for the purposes of the Act?

Common law rules apply
The 1957 Act does not define what constitutes an occupier
but stipulates that the rules of the common law shall apply:
s 1(2).

The test is one of control and not exclusive occupation
The basic test for an occupier is one of control over the
premises. There can also be more than one occupier of
premises, at any given time: *Wheat v E Lacon & Co Ltd* (1966).
The defendants owned a public house and the manager and
his wife occupied the upper floor. The manager's wife was
allowed to take paying guests and one of these guests had
an accident on the staircase leading to the upper floor. It was
held that the defendants were occupiers of the upper floor
as they exercised residuary control.

It is not necessary to be present on the premises
In *Harris v Birkenhead Corporation* (1976), the local authority had issued a notice of compulsory purchase order and notice of entry but had not taken possession. They were held to be occupiers.

Who is a 'visitor' for the purposes of the Act?

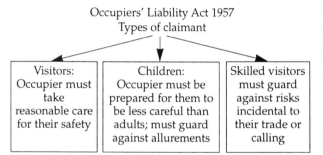

Occupiers' Liability Act 1957
Types of claimant

Visitors: Occupier must take reasonable care for their safety	Children: Occupier must be prepared for them to be less careful than adults; must guard against allurements	Skilled visitors must guard against risks incidental to their trade or calling

General category of visitor
The Act replaces the old common law distinctions between 'invitees' and 'licensees' and replaces it with a general category of 'visitor'.

Express and implied permission
A visitor is someone who has express or implied permission to be on the land. So, either someone who has been expressly requested to enter onto premises or has permission to be there.

- *Knowledge of presence does not imply permission.* The fact that the occupier knows of the plaintiff's presence or has failed to take steps to prevent entry does not mean that the occupier has given a licence: *Edwards v Railway Executive* (1952).

- *Rules the same for children but may be a tacit licence.* Knowledge that a track is constantly used by children together with a failure to take any steps to indicate that passage is not permitted does amount to a tacit licence: *Lowery v Walker* (1911).

- *Entering premises to communicate with occupier does amount to tacit licence.* A person entering with the purpose of communicating with the occupier will have implied permission, for example, asking directions, the postman, roundsman, etc.

- *Entering premises to exercise a right conferred by law amounts to licence.* Section 2(6) stipulates that anyone entering premises for any purpose in the exercise of a right conferred by law, are visitors, for example, police with search warrants and officials empowered by statute to enter premises.

- *Exercising a public right of way does not constitute a licence.* A person exercising a public right of way has no claim under the 1957 Act because such a person was not an 'invitee' or 'licensee' at common law.

  In *Greenhalgh v British Railway Board* (1969), a railway bridge was built by the defendant's predecessor in title in 1873. In 1950, a housing estate was built either side of the railway bridge and the bridge was used to connect the two. The plaintiff was injured when he stepped into a pothole. It was held that the plaintiff was exercising a right of way and was not a 'visitor'.

- *National Parks and Access to the Countryside Act 1949.* Exercising rights under the National Parks and Countryside Act 1949 does not confer the status of a visitor.

The common duty of care

The 1957 Act states that a common duty of care is owed by an occupier to all visitors except insofar as he has extended, restricted, excluded or modified his duty.

The common duty of care is the duty to take such care as is reasonable to see that the visitor will be reasonably safe in using the premises for the purpose for which he is invited by the occupier to be there: s 2(2).

The defendant was held liable under s 2 in *Cunningham v Reading FC* (1992) for negligently permitting the concrete structure of its ground to fall into disrepair so that rioting fans could break lumps off and use them as missiles.

Standard of care. The same standard of care as that which applies in ordinary negligence applies.

Guidelines. The 1957 Act provides guidelines in the application of the common duty of care. Section 2(3) provides that the circumstances relevant for the purpose include the degree of care and want of care, which would ordinarily be looked for in such a visitor, so that (for example) in proper cases:

- an occupier must be prepared for children to be less careful than adults;
- an occupier must expect that a person, in the exercise of his calling, will appreciate against any special risks ordinarily incident to his trade or calling.

Children

An occupier must be prepared for children to be less careful than adults. In *Moloney v Lambeth LBC* (1966), the occupier was liable when a four year old boy fell through a gap in railings protecting a stairwell, when an adult could not have fallen through the gap.

- *Allurements.* An occupier must take precautions against children being attracted by allurements. In *Glasgow Corporation v Taylor* (1922), a seven year old boy ate poisonous berries on a visit to a botanical garden. It was held that the occupiers were liable as they knew that the berries were poisonous and they had made no attempt to fence the berries off.

- *Definition of Allurements.* Allurements were defined by Hamilton LJ in *Latham v R Johnson and Nephew Ltd* (1913) as something involving the idea of 'concealment and surprise, of an appearance of safety under circumstances cloaking a reality of danger'. So, in that the case of a child playing with a heap of stones had no remedy, as stones do not involve any element of allurement. In *Jolley v London Borough of Sutton* (1998), the Court of Appeal ruled that a boat in a dangerous condition was an allurement to a 14 year old.

  In *Phipps v Rochester Corporation* (1955), a trench that was not concealed was held not to be an allurement and, in *Simkiss v Rhondda BC* (1983), there was no concealed danger in sliding down a steep bluff on a blanket.

The concept of 'allurement' does not make the occupier liable for unforeseeable risks. In *Jolley v Sutton LBC* (1998), the occupier had left a boat on land which was a trap and attraction for children. The occupier was only liable for those injuries which were reasonably foreseeable. So, although it was foreseeable that children would play on an abandoned boat and might injure themselves on it, it was not foreseeable that older children would attempt to repair the boat by jacking it up. Consequently, the occupier was not liable when the jacked up boat fell on a boy and injured him.

Skilled visitors

An occupier is entitled to expect that a person in the exercise of his calling will appreciate and guard against any special risks incidental to his trade.

In *Roles v Nathan* (1963), two chimney sweeps died from carbon monoxide poisoning while cleaning the flue of a boiler. They had been warned not to continue working while the boiler was alight. The occupier was held not to be liable as, firstly, they had been warned of the danger and, secondly, it was reasonable to expect a specialist to appreciate and guard against the dangers arising from the very defect that he had been called in to deal with.

- *The risk must be incidental to the trade or calling.* In *Bird v King Line Ltd* (1970), it was held that the risks of working on a ship did not include falling on refuse which was carelessly left on the deck.

- *Occupier liability to skilled rescuers.* In *Ogwo v Taylor* (1988), the occupier negligently started a fire and was liable to a fireman injured in the fire where the fire fighting operation has been carried out with due care.

Independent contractors

It will be a defence for the occupier to show that the defective state of the premises is caused by the faulty execution of work of construction, repair or maintenance by an independent contractor provided that (s 2(4)(b)):

Reasonable to entrust work to a contractor

It depends on the circumstances whether it was reasonable to entrust the work to a contractor and the nature of the work to be done.

```
┌─────────────────────────┐        ┌─────────────────────────┐
│  It was reasonable to   │        │  The occupier had taken │
│  entrust the work to an │        │  reasonable care to see │
│  independent contractor │        │    that the contractor  │
│                         │        │       was competent     │
└─────────────────────────┘        └─────────────────────────┘
              ↖                          ↗
                      Defences
                         │
                         ↓
              ┌─────────────────────────┐
              │   The occupier had taken│
              │  reasonable care to check│
              │    that the work was    │
              │     reasonably done     │
              └─────────────────────────┘
```

The more complex the work the more reasonable it will be
to entrust it to a contractor. Thus, in *Haseldine v CA Daw &
Son Ltd* (1941), an occupier was not liable for the negligence
of an independent contractor in maintaining a lift in a block
of flats. This can be contrasted with *Woodward v Mayor of
Hastings* (1945) where the occupiers were liable for the
negligence of a cleaner in leaving a step in an icy condition.
Cleaning a step does not require any particular skill.

Discharge of the duty of care

Warning
Section 2(4)(a) provides that an occupier can discharge his
duty to a visitor by giving a warning of the danger that in all
the circumstances allows the visitor to be reasonably safe.

The test for determining whether a warning was adequate is
a subjective one. A written warning will not be adequate in
the case of someone who is blind or cannot read or speak
English.

In *Staples v West Dorset District Council* (1995), it was held that an occupier had not been negligent when the Council had failed to provide a warning and the danger was obvious. In such circumstances, a warning would not have told the visitor anything he did not already know and would not have affected his conduct.

Acceptance of the risk

Section 2(5) provides that an occupier does not have an obligation to a visitor in respect of risks willingly accepted by the visitor.

In *Simms v Leigh Rugby Football Club Ltd* (1969), the plaintiff had accepted the risks of playing on a rugby league ground which conformed to the byelaws of the Rugby League.

- *Knowledge of specific risk*. In *White v Blackmore* (1972), it was held that it was insufficient to show that the plaintiff knew that jalopy car racing was dangerous; it was necessary to show that the plaintiff had consented to the specific risk that made that particular track dangerous.

Exclusion of liability

Section 2(1) provides that an occupier is able to 'exclude, restrict or modify his duty'. In *Ashdown v Samuel Williams & Sons Ltd* (1957), the Court of Appeal accepted that a notice was sufficient to exclude liability. In *White v Blackmore* (1972), notices put at the entrance to the field were sufficient to exclude liability.

- *Unfair Contract Terms Act 1977*. The Unfair Contract Terms Act (UCTA) has greatly restricted the occupier's ability to exclude his liability.

- *Premises used for business premises*. As far as premises used for business purposes are concerned, the occupier is unable to exclude liability for death and personal injury.

Exclusion of liability for other types of loss must satisfy the reasonableness test contained in s 7 of UCTA.

- *Premises used for private purposes.* Occupiers of premises which are not in business use can only exclude liability if such exclusion is reasonable.

- *Remoteness.* The test for remoteness under the 1957 Act is the same that applies to a common law action for negligence (*Jolley v Sutton London Borough Council* (1998)).

Occupiers' liability to trespassers

Common law rule
At common law, the original rule was that there was a mere duty not to deliberately or recklessly injure a trespasser: *Addie v Dumbreck* (1929). There was a change of policy in the case of *British Railways Board v Herrington* (1972) when it was held that an occupier was under a duty to act humanely towards trespassers. This was owed when a reasonable man knowing the physical facts which the occupier actually knew would appreciate that a trespasser's presence at the point and time of danger was so likely that, in all the circumstances, it would be inhumane not to give effective warning of the danger.

Occupiers' Liability Act 1984
The Occupiers' Liability Act 1984 replaces the common law to determine whether an occupier owes a duty to persons other than visitors.

Under s 1(3), a duty is owed by the occupier if:

  (a) he is aware of the danger or has reasonable grounds to believe that it exists;
  (b) he knows or has reasonable grounds to believe that the other person is in the vicinity of the

> danger concerned, or that he may come into the
> vicinity of danger (in either case, whether the
> other has lawful authority for being in the vicinity
> or not); and
>
> (c) the risk is one against which in all the
> circumstances of the case he may reasonably be
> expected to offer the other some protection.

Issues relating to the Occupiers' Liability Act 1984 arose in the case of *Revill v Newberry* (1995). The plaintiff was a trespasser attempting to break into a brick shed on an allotment belonging to the defendant. The defendant poked a shotgun through a small hole in the door and fired, injuring the plaintiff. The defendant had no means of knowing whether anyone was standing in front of the door. The plaintiff brought a claim in assault; under s 1 of the Occupiers' Liability Act 1984 and negligence. The claim for assault was dropped. Neill LJ held that the Occupiers' Liability Act 1984 did not apply. The defendant was not being sued in his capacity as occupier with regard to the safety of the premises. The case had to be decided in accordance with the ordinary principles of negligence.

In *Ratcliffe v McConnell* (1998), the Court of Appeal decided that a student who was seriously injured when he dived into a swimming pool at 2 am when it was locked had consented to run the risk of injury under s 1(6) of the 1984 Act.

Discharge of the duty

Warning
Section 1(5) provides that the duty may be discharged by taking such steps as are reasonable in all the circumstances to warn of the danger concerned, or to discourage persons from incurring risk.

In *Cotton v Derbyshire Dales District Council* (1994), it was held that there was no duty to warn against dangers that are obvious.

Exclusion of liability

The 1984 Act is silent on the question whether the duty can be excluded with regard to trespassers. It has been argued that it is not possible to exclude a liability to a trespasser as it is a minimal duty.

Occupiers' liability

```
        ┌─────────────────────────────┐
        │  Is the entrant a visitor or a │
        │         trespasser?          │
        └─────────────────────────────┘
              │                    │
      ┌───────┘                    └───────┐
      ▼                                    ▼
┌──────────────┐                    ┌──────────────┐
│  Trespasser  │                    │   Visitor    │
└──────────────┘                    └──────────────┘
      │                                    │
      ▼                                    ▼
┌──────────────────┐            ┌──────────────────────┐
│ Was the occupier │            │  Is the visitor a     │
│ aware or should  │            │  child/skilled        │
│ have been aware  │            │  entrant/unskilled    │
│ of the danger?   │            │  adult entrant        │
└──────────────────┘            └──────────────────────┘
      │                                    │
      ▼                                    ▼
┌──────────────────┐            ┌──────────────────────┐
│ Was the occupier │            │ Duty to ensure that   │
│ aware/should the │            │ the visitor is        │
│ occupier have    │            │ reasonably safe,      │
│ been aware of    │            │ to be aware that a    │
│ trespassers?     │            │ child is less careful │
└──────────────────┘            │ than an adult and to  │
      │                         │ guard against         │
      ▼                         │ allurements           │
┌──────────────────┐            └──────────────────────┘
│ Has the occupier │                       │
│ done what is     │                       ▼
│ reasonably       │            ┌──────────────────────┐
│ practicable?     │            │ Has the occupier      │
└──────────────────┘            │ provided a warning?   │
                                └──────────────────────┘
                                           │
                                           ▼
                                ┌──────────────────────┐
                                │ Has the occupier      │
                                │ excluded/modified/    │
                                │ restricted duty?      │
                                │ Note the Unfair       │
                                │ Contract Terms Act    │
                                └──────────────────────┘
```

3 Torts relating to land

Private nuisance

Bases of liability:			
Negligence	Private nuisance	Public nuisance	*Rylands v Fletcher*(1868)
Fault: breach of duty which caused injury	Fault: unreasonable use of land	Can be a tort of strict liability *Wringe v Cohen* (1940); *Tarry v Ashton* (1876); otherwise interference with rights of public	Strict liability

The relationship between private nuisance and public nuisance

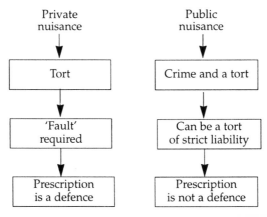

There tends to be confusion between public and private nuisance. Public nuisance is a crime covering a number of interferences with rights of the public at large such as brothel keeping, selling impure food and obstructing public highways. It is not tortious unless an individual proves that he has suffered particular damage beyond that suffered by the rest of the community.

Private nuisance is an unlawful interference with the use or enjoyment of land or some right over or in connection with it.

At one time, the law of private nuisance seemed to be moving away from solely restraining activities which affected enjoyment of land. In *Khorasandijan v Bush* (1993), the plaintiff was granted an injunction not only in respect of harassing telephone calls at home but also for harassment at work and in the street.

The House of Lords in *Hunter v Canary Wharf* (1997) rejected this approach and confined nuisance to its traditional boundaries. Lord Hoffman emphasised, in that case, that it is a tort relating to land.

However, private nuisance has been held to extend to damage to a floating barge moored in a river (*Crown River Cruises Ltd v Kimbolton Fireworks Ltd* (1996)). Since the barge was in use as a mooring, it was so attached for the purpose of the better use and enjoyment of the plaintiffs' mooring right and, therefore, sufficient to sustain an action for private nuisance.

Public nuisance is different from private nuisance as it is not necessarily connected with the user of land. Public nuisance is usually a crime although it can be a tort. To make matters even more confusing, the same incident can be both a public and a private nuisance.

Types of private nuisance

Private nuisance is an unlawful interference with the use or enjoyment of land, or some right over or in connection with it.

What is unlawful falls to be decided in an *ex post facto* manner. Most activities which give rise to claims in nuisance are in themselves lawful. It is only when the activity interferes with another's enjoyment of land to an extent that it is a nuisance that it becomes unlawful.

Examples of private nuisance

It was said by Lord Wright that 'the forms that nuisance take are protean'. Examples would be as follows:

(a) Encroachment on the plaintiff's land: *Davey v Harrow Corporation* (1958).

(b) Physical damage to the plaintiff's land: *Sedleigh-Denfield v O'Callaghan* (1940).

(c) Interference with the plaintiff's use or enjoyment of land through smells, smoke, dust, noise, etc: *Halsey v Esso Petroleum Co Ltd* (1961).

(d) Interference with an easement or profit.

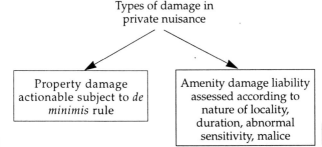

Types of damage in private nuisance

Property damage actionable subject to *de minimis* rule

Amenity damage liability assessed according to nature of locality, duration, abnormal sensitivity, malice

Physical damage

As a general rule, nuisance is not actionable *per se* and actual damage must be proved, subject to the following exceptions:

- where a presumption of damage can be made, for example, by building a cornice so that it projects over the land of the plaintiff, it may be presumed that damage will be caused to the land of the plaintiff by rain water dripping from the cornice onto the land;

- interference with an easement, *profit à prendre* or right of access where there has been acquiescence in certain circumstances.

So, private nuisance is concerned with balancing the competing claims of neighbours to use their property as they think fit. However, a distinction must be made between physical damage to property, where such conduct will, subject to the *de minimis* rule, be a nuisance and personal discomfort or amenity damage, where the judge will consider many factors to determine the balance.

If the conduct complained of causes physical damage to the plaintiff's property, this will amount to nuisance (subject to any defence available). In *St Helens Smelting Co v Tipping* (1865), Lord Westbury said an 'occupier is entitled to expect protection from physical damage no matter where he lives'.

Amenity damage

Amenity damage is interference such as noise, smells, dust and vibrations which will interfere with use and enjoyment of land without physically damaging the property.

In the case of amenity damage, the degree of interference has to be measured against the surrounding circumstances.

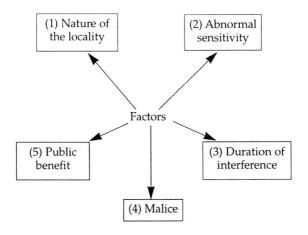

(1) Nature of the locality. This is an important determinant of what constitutes nuisance in the case of amenity damage. As was said in *St Helens Smelting Co v Tipping* (1865), 'one should not expect the clean air of the Lake District in an industrial town such as St Helens'. The plaintiff's estate was located in a manufacturing area. Fumes from a copper smelting works damaged the trees on the estate. The distinction was made between physical damage and amenity damage, particularly the nature of the surrounding area and locality.

Interesting questions of locality were raised in *Halsey v Esso Petroleum Co* (1961). The plaintiff's house was in a zone that was classified as residential for planning purposes. The defendant's oil depot was across the road in an industrial zone.

There was a combination of physical and amenity damage:

- acid smuts from the defendant's depot damaged paintwork on the plaintiff's car, clothing and washing on the line;

- there was a nauseating smell;

- noise from the boilers caused the plaintiff's windows and doors to vibrate and prevented him from sleeping. There was also noise from the delivery tankers at night.

The damage to the clothing on washing line etc constituted physical damage and was recoverable. Before allowing recovery for the intangible damage, the locality had to be taken into account. Trifling inconveniences were disregarded but the locality set the measure of what was acceptable and the interference substantially exceeded the standards of the surrounding neighbourhood.

In *Laws v Florinplace Ltd* (1981), the defendants opened a sex centre and cinema club which showed explicit sex acts. Local residents sought an injunction. It was held that the use constituted a private nuisance.

Similarly, in *Thompson-Schwab v Costaki* (1956), the plaintiff lived in a respectable residential street in the West End of London. The defendant used a house in the same street for the purposes of prostitution. It was held that, having regard to the character of the neighbourhood, the defendant's use of the property constituted a nuisance.

However, the character of a neighbourhood can change over the years, and a more modern approach is for the court to ask whether the acts complained of are more than can be tolerated in modern living conditions. If so, they will constitute a nuisance: *Blackburn v ARC Ltd* (1998).

In the public nuisance case of *Gillingham BC v Medway (Chatham) Dock Co* (1993), it was held that the nature of a locality can be changed through planning permission.

In *Wheeler v Saunders* (1995), it was held that a local authority had no jurisdiction to authorise a nuisance save in so far as it had the power to permit a change in the character of the neighbourhood and the nuisance resulted inevitably from the change of use.

In *Murdoch v Glacier Metal Co Ltd* (1998), excess noise from a nearby factory above World Health Organisation levels was not actionable nuisance. Allowance had to be made for the character of the neighbourhood which was next to a busy by-pass.

(2) *Abnormal sensitivity*. Personal discomfort is not to be judged by the standards of the plaintiff but must be made by reference to the standards of any ordinary person who might occupy the plaintiff's property. It must be an 'inconvenience materially interfering with the ordinary comfort physically of human existence, not merely according to elegant and dainty modes and habits of living but according to plain and sober and simple notions among the English people', *per* Knight Bruce VC in *Walter v Selfe* (1851).

Consequently, a vicar who was put off his sermons in *Heath v Mayor of Brighton* (1908) by a low hum from the defendant's electricity works was being abnormally sensitive particularly as he had been the only person annoyed and it had not stopped anyone from attending church.

- *Abnormal sensitivity and physical damage*. In the same way, a defendant will not be liable for physical damage to property caused because of its exceptionally delicate nature. A man cannot increase the liabilities of his neighbour by applying his own property to special uses.

In *Robinson v Kilvert* (1889), the plaintiff occupied a basement in the ground floor of the defendant's building and stored brown paper there. The defendant's boiler had an adverse effect on the plaintiff's goods, although it wouldn't have affected any other type of paper. The plaintiff failed to get an injunction because of the exceptionally delicate trade that he was carrying on.

• *Changing nature of use. Bridlington Relay Ltd v Yorkshire Electricity Board* (1965) is an illustration of how ideas of exceptionally delicate trade might change. The plaintiffs were in business relaying sound and television broadcasts and the defendant's power lines interfered with their transmissions. It was held that the plaintiffs were carrying on an exceptionally delicate trade.

For some time, it was thought that *Bridlington Relay Ltd* would be decided differently, if it was decided today. Not least because television ownership has become much more widespread since the case was decided.

However, in *Hunter v Canary Wharf* (1997), the presence of the Canary Wharf tower interfered with the plaintiffs' television reception but the House of Lords held that they could not succeed in private nuisance. It was not ruled out that interference with television could never be actionable nuisance, at present it seems unlikely.

On the other hand, if the defendants activities would have interfered with the ordinary use of the land, he will be liable notwithstanding the plaintiff's abnormal sensitivity. In *Mackinnon Industries Ltd v Walker* (1951), the Privy Council held that once substantial interference is proved, the remedies for interference will extend to a sensitive and delicate operation.

(3) *Duration of interference*. Interference of a temporary or occasional nature may cause annoyance, but an injunction will rarely be granted. The temporary duration of the alleged nuisance is one factor to be taken into account and the judge will conclude that it is the price of social existence that neighbours suffer temporary annoyance at various times, such as during building or renovation.

The defendant in *Swaine v GN Railway* (1864) dumped refuse next to the plaintiff's property before moving onto another property. The plaintiff's claim in nuisance failed as it was temporary and occasional.

- *Grave temporary interference*. The courts will allow actions for temporary nuisance where the interference is grave. So, in *Mantania v National Provincial Bank* (1936), the plaintiff succeeded when a temporary nuisance, in the form of building works carried on by the defendant's independent contractors, prevented the plaintiff from carrying on his livelihood, as a music teacher.

  Similarly, in *De Keyser's Royal Hotel v Spicer Bros* (1914), use of a steam pile driving machine outside the plaintiff's hotel causing hotel guests to lose a nights sleep and the prevention of after dinner speakers from making themselves heard also constituted nuisance.

  Contrast the *De Keyser's Royal Hotel* case with *Murdoch v Glacier Metal Co Ltd* (1998) where excess noise from a nearby factory which exceeded World Health Organisation levels was not actionable nuisance. The property was in a noisy neighbourhood.

- *Single act of the defendant*. Nuisance is usually associated with a continuing state of affairs rather than a single act of the defendant. It was held in *British Celanese Ltd v AH*

Hunt (Capacitors) Ltd (1969) that an isolated occurrence could constitute nuisance.

In *SCM (UK) Ltd v WJ Whittal & Son Ltd* (1970), it was held that a single escape could constitute nuisance; the nuisance must arise from the condition of the defendant's land. It should be remembered that a single occurrence could constitute a right of action under the rule in *Rylands v Fletcher* (1868).

(4) *Malice*. Motive is generally irrelevant in tort, as can be seen from *Bradford Corporation v Pickles* (1895) where a bad motive on its own did not create a right of action.

This rule needs qualification in the case of private nuisance, as malice may tip the scales in the defendant's favour and conduct, which would not otherwise be actionable, becomes unlawful and a nuisance if it has been committed maliciously. In *Christie v Davey* (1893), the defendant lived next door to a music teacher. He objected to the noise and retaliated with banging on the walls, beating trays etc. The plaintiff was granted an injunction but the outcome would have been different if the acts had been innocent.

In *Hollywood Silver Fox Farm Ltd v Emmett* (1936), the plaintiffs bred silver foxes. If they are disturbed in the breeding season they eat their young. The defendant fired a gun as near as possible to the breeding pens with the malicious intention of causing damage. The defendant was held liable although the decision has been criticised on the grounds that the silver foxes were an exceptionally delicate trade. It seems that the element of malice was sufficient to alter the outcome.

(5) *Public benefit*. It is not a defence in nuisance to say that the activity is being carried on in the public benefit: *Adams v*

Ursell (1913). Nevertheless, if the activity is being carried out for the good of the community in general, then the courts are more likely to find the use of the land as reasonable.

Defendant's negligence

The fact that a defendant has acted with all reasonable care does not necessarily mean that the use of the land was reasonable and therefore constitutes nuisance. On the other hand, want of reasonable care may be strong evidence of a nuisance. It is not reasonable to expect a plaintiff to endure discomfort which the defendant could have avoided with reasonable care.

Lord Reid in *The Wagon Mound* (1967) said that '... negligence in the narrow sense may not be necessary, but fault of some kind is almost always necessary, and generally involves foreseeability'.

As nuisance is a tort which relates to use of land, fault in nuisance is thought to relate to unreasonable use of land. This makes fault in nuisance an altogether more subjective concept in nuisance than in negligence. Nuisance does not use the same concepts for assessing fault as negligence. It does not require the existence of a duty of care before establishing the existence of fault but, confusingly, judges have used the terminology of negligence when discussing nuisance. However, foreseeability that an act of nature will cause nuisance can make use of the land unreasonable: *Leakey v National Trust* (1980); *Goldman v Hargrave* (1967).

Nuisance is also distinct from negligence in terms of who has *locus standi* to bring an action and the remedies available.

Liability has been imposed in public nuisance in the absence of fault: *Tarry v Ashton* (1876); *Wringe v Cohen* (1940).

Who can sue?

Nuisance protects those persons who have an interest in the land affected, so only an owner or occupier with an interest in the land can sue.

The plaintiff in *Khorasandijan v Bush* succeeded without having a proprietary interest in the land. She was being harassed by a former boyfriend. Most of the harassment took place at her mother's home, in which the plaintiff had no proprietary interest. Dillon LJ said that the law had to be re-considered in the light of changed social conditions. He felt that as the mother could have sued, then there is no reason to prevent the daughter suing.

Khorasandijan illustrates an expansionary approach to the tort of nuisance. It was decided at a time when it appeared that it would evolve to protect interests other than land. The case was overruled by *Hunter v Canary Wharf* (1997). The majority of the House of Lords held that the plaintiff should establish a right to the land affected in order to sue in private nuisance. This restricts nuisance as a tort designed to protect interests in land.

In cases of harassment such as *Khorasandijan*, the House of Lords suggested that plaintiffs proceed under different causes of action. The rights of action mentioned were negligence, the rule in *Wilkinson v Downton* and the Protection from Harassment Act 1997.

The 1997 Act creates civil remedies and criminal offences in respect of 'a course of conduct which amounts to harassment' which the defendant 'knows or ought to know amounts to harassment'. Conduct will be regarded as harassing if a reasonable person in possession of the same information thought that it was harassing.

In *Malone v Laskey* (1907), the wife of a licensee whose enjoyment of the land was interfered with could not sue in nuisance, as she did not have a proprietary interest.

Who can be sued?

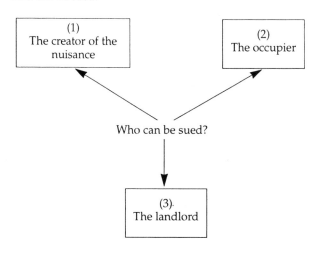

```
┌──────────────────┐          ┌──────────────────┐
│       (1)        │          │       (2)        │
│ The creator of the│          │  The occupier    │
│    nuisance      │          │                  │
└──────────────────┘          └──────────────────┘
           ↖                    ↗
              Who can be sued?
                    │
                    ↓
           ┌──────────────────┐
           │       (3).        │
           │  The landlord    │
           └──────────────────┘
```

(1) The creator of the nuisance
A person who creates a nuisance by positive conduct may be sued. It is not necessary for the creator of the nuisance to have any interest in the land from which the nuisance emanates.

In the words of Devlin J in *Southport Corporation v Esso* (1954): 'I can see no reason why … if the defendant as a licensee or trespasser misuses someone else's land, he should not be liable for a nuisance in the same way as an adjoining occupier would be.'

(2) The occupier

The occupier is the usual defendant in private nuisance. An occupier will be liable for:

- *Persons under his control.* Under the principles of agency and vicarious liability.

- *Independent contractors.* Where nuisance is an inevitable or foreseeable consequence of work undertaken by independent contractors, the occupier cannot avoid liability by employing a contractor as in the case of *Mantania v National Provincial Bank Ltd* (1936).

- *Actions of a predecessor in title.* An occupier who knows or ought reasonably to have known of the existence of a predecessor in title will be liable for continuing the nuisance if he does not abate it. If the nuisance could not reasonably have been discovered, he will not be liable.

  It was held in *St Anne's Well Brewery Co v Roberts* (1929) that if, at the date of a letting, the landlord knows or ought to know of the condition giving rise to the actionable nuisance, then he is liable during the tenancy where he does not take from the tenant a covenant to repair.

- *Actions of trespassers.* An occupier is not liable for a nuisance created on his land by a trespasser unless he adopts or continues the nuisance.

  In *Sedleigh-Denfield v O'Callaghan* (1940), the boundary between the appellant's premises and those of the respondents was a hedge and a ditch, both of which belonged to the respondents. Without informing the respondents, a trespasser laid a pipe in the ditch and some three years later the pipe became blocked and the appellant's garden was flooded. The respondents' servants had cleared the ditch out twice yearly. The appellants claimed damages in nuisance.

It was held that he would succeed because the respondents knew or ought to have known of the existence of the nuisance and permitted it to continue without taking prompt and efficient action to abate it.

- *Acts of nature*. At common law, it was thought that an occupier had no duty to abate a nuisance that arose on his land from natural causes. The extent of the obligation was to permit his neighbour access to abate the nuisance. The Privy Council in *Goldman v Hargrave* (1967) established that an occupier is under a duty to do what is reasonable in the circumstances to prevent or minimise a known risk of damage to the neighbour's property.

The appellant was the owner/occupier of land next to the respondents. A tree on the appellant's land was struck by lightning and caught fire. The appellants took steps to deal with the burning tree but subsequently left the fire to burn itself out and took no steps to prevent the fire spreading. The fire later revived and spread causing extensive damage to the respondent's land. The appellants were held to be liable.

In *Leakey v National Trust* (1980), the defendants owned a hill that was liable to crack and slip. The plaintiffs owned houses at the foot of the hill. After a large fall the plaintiffs asked the defendants to remove the earth and debris from their land but they refused saying they were not responsible for what had occurred. The defendants were held liable in nuisance. It was reasonable to prevent or minimise the known risk of damage or injury to one's neighbour or to his property.

In *Bradburn v Lindsay* (1983), it was held that where houses have mutual rights of support, negligently allowing property to fall into dereliction so as to damage the adjoining premises is actionable in negligence as well as in nuisance.

(3) The landlord
A landlord may be liable for a nuisance arising in three types of situation:

(a) Where the landlord authorised the nuisance. In *Sampson v Hodson* (1981), a tiled terrace was built over the plaintiff's sitting room and bedroom. The noise was excessive and it was held that the landlord was liable in nuisance.

A landlord, who let flats with poor sound insulation to tenants, was not liable in the tort of nuisance to a tenant whose reasonable use and enjoyment of her flat was interfered with by the ordinary use of an adjoining flat by another tenant (*Baxter v Camden London Borough Council (No 2)* (1998)).

It is arguable that a landowner can be liable for repeated acts constituting nuisance committed from its land by those it knew were in occupation, and where no steps were taken to evict them (*Lippiatt v South Gloucestershire City Council* (1999)).

However, all will depend on the exact circumstances and in *Hussein v Lancaster CC* (1998), the Court of Appeal found that a local authority was not liable for failing to stop acts of criminal damage by council tenants where the harassment did not emanate from 'common parts' of an estate, such as walkways and avenues. In this case, a claim in negligence also failed an application of the test in *Caparo v Dickman*.

(b) Nuisance existed before the date of the letting.

(c) Where the landlord has an obligation or right to repair.

The law on landlords' liability for nuisance is still developing and there are conflicting lines of authority which can be confusing – see Court of Appeal in *Southwark London BC v Mills* (1998).

Defences

Prescription
A defendant who has carried on an activity for 20 years may claim a prescriptive right to commit the nuisance. The activity must be an actionable nuisance for the entire 20 year period.

In *Sturges v Bridgeman* (1879), a confectioner and a physician lived next door to each other. The confectioner used two large machines and had done so for more than 20 years. The noise and vibrations had been no problem until the physician built a consulting room at the end of his garden. It was held that the confectioner could not rely on the defence of prescription as there was no actionable nuisance until the consulting room had been built.

Statutory authority
If a statute authorises the defendants' activity, the defendants will not be liable for interferences which are inevitable and could not have been avoided by the exercise of reasonable care.

In *Allen v Gulf Oil Refining Ltd* (1981), a statute authorised the defendants to carry out oil refinement works. The plaintiff complained of noise, smell and vibration. It was held that the defendants had a defence of statutory immunity.

It is *not* a defence to plead:

(1) The plaintiff moved to the nuisance: *Sturges v Bridgeman*

In *Miller v Jackson* (1977), cricket had been played on a village ground since 1905. In 1970, houses were built in such a place that cricket balls went into a garden. It was held that there was a nuisance; there was an interference with the reasonable enjoyment of land. It was no defence to say the plaintiff had brought trouble onto his own head by moving there.

In *Baxter v Camden London Borough Council (No. 2)* (1998) it was held that *Sturges v Bridgeman* does not apply where the parties are landlord and tenant. Such cases were decided on the principle 'caveat lessee' and the lessee was bound to take the premises as he found them.

(2) That there is a substantial public benefit

In *Adams v Ursell* (1913), the defendant ran a fish and chip shop. The plaintiff objected to the noise and smells. The defendant tried to argue that the fish and chip shop was of public benefit but it was held that this was no defence.

(3) That the nuisance is the result of the separate actions of several people

In *Pride of Derby and Derbyshire Angling Association Ltd v British Celanese Ltd* (1953), pollutant sewage from factories reached a river through the effluent pipe of a local authority from the sewage works. It was held that the local authority was responsible.

Abatement or self-help

Notice should be given except in an emergency
or where it is not necessary to
enter the wrongdoer's land

In *Co-operative Wholesale Society Limited v British Railways Board* (1995), it was held that the right to abatement was confined to cases where the security of lives and property required immediate and speedy action or where such action could be exercised simply without recourse to the expense and inconvenience of legal proceedings in circumstances unlikely to give rise to argument or dispute. Where an application to court could be made, the remedy of self help was neither appropriate or desirable.

Damages

Lord Hoffman in *Hunter v Canary Wharf* (1997) said that damages should be fixed by reference to the diminution to the capital value of the property.

Remedies for
private nuisance

Injunction

An injunction is an equitable and therefore a discretionary remedy.

If the injunction is a continuing one the plaintiff will be granted an injunction except:

(a) if the injury to the plaintiff's legal rights is small
(b) and is one capable of being estimated in money
(c) and is one adequately compensated by a small money payment
(d) and is a case where it would be oppressive to the defendants to grant an injunction

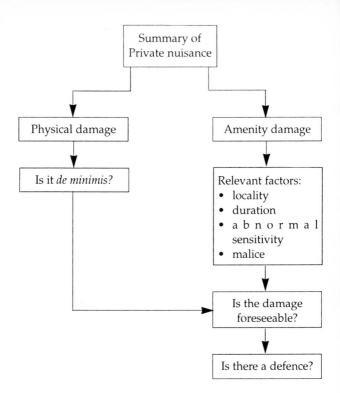

```
            ┌─────────────────┐
            │   Summary of    │
            │ Private nuisance│
            └────────┬────────┘
         ┌───────────┴───────────┐
         ▼                       ▼
┌─────────────────┐     ┌─────────────────┐
│ Physical damage │     │ Amenity damage  │
└────────┬────────┘     └────────┬────────┘
         ▼                       ▼
┌─────────────────┐     ┌─────────────────┐
│ Is it de minimis?│    │ Relevant factors:│
└────────┬────────┘     │ • locality       │
         │              │ • duration       │
         │              │ • a b n o r m a l │
         │              │   sensitivity    │
         │              │ • malice         │
         │              └────────┬────────┘
         │                       ▼
         │              ┌─────────────────┐
         └─────────────▶│ Is the damage   │
                        │ foreseeable?    │
                        └────────┬────────┘
                                 ▼
                        ┌─────────────────┐
                        │ Is there a      │
                        │ defence?        │
                        └─────────────────┘
```

Public nuisance

A public nuisance is a crime as well as a tort. The remedy for a public nuisance is a prosecution or relator action by the Attorney General on behalf of the public. A plaintiff who suffers particular damage, over and above the damage suffered by the rest of the public, may maintain an action in public nuisance. Public nuisance has been defined as 'an act or omission which materially affects the reasonable comfort of a class of Her Majesty's subjects', *per* Romer LJ in *AG v PYA Quarries Ltd* (1957).

Public nuisance is most important in relation to highways

What obstructions are actionable?
- A temporary or permanent obstruction that is reasonable in amount and duration will not be a nuisance.

  In *Russell* (1805), the defendant left wagons standing on the street for several hours at a time for the purpose of loading and unloading and this was held to be a public nuisance.

  In *AG v Gastonia Coaches Ltd* (1977), overnight parking of coaches in the street constituted a nuisance.

- An obstruction which creates a foreseeable danger will amount to a nuisance.

  In *Ware v Garston Haulage Co* (1944), an unlit vehicle parked at night so as to obstruct the highway may cause a nuisance, although it will depend on the facts.

  In *Dymond v Pearce* (1972), the defendant parked a lorry overnight under a lit street lamp without lights. This was regarded as a nuisance although the plaintiff did not succeed as the nuisance was not the cause of the plaintiff's injury.

Premises adjoining the highway
Tarry v Ashton (1876) is an example of public nuisance being capable of a tort of strict liability. The defendant's lamp projected over the highway. An independent contractor repaired the lamp but it fell on the plaintiff. The defendant was found liable in the absence of fault.

Similarly, in *Wringe v Cohen* (1940), a wall to the defendants' houses which were let to weekly tenants collapsed. The defendants, who were liable to keep the house in a good state of repair, did not know that the wall was in a dangerous condition but was nevertheless held to be liable. In *Mint v Good* (1951), again, a wall in front of houses which were let to weekly tenants collapsed although there was no express agreement between the landlord and tenant as to repair. The landlord was held to be liable.

Does the occupier have to be aware of the nuisance?

In *Shorrock* (1994), the defendant let a farm on his field to three persons for a weekend for £2,000. The defendant did not know the purpose for which the field had been let. The field was used for an acid house party lasting 15 hours and attended by between 3,000 and 5,000 people who paid £15 per person admission. Many local people complained about the noise and disturbance caused by the party and the defendant and the organisers were charged with public nuisance.

It was held that it was not necessary to show that the defendant had actual knowledge of the nuisance but merely that he knew or ought to have known the consequences of activities carried out on his land. The defendant ought to have known that there was a real risk that the consequences of the licence would create the nuisance that occurred.

Nature of the locality

Where there has been planning consent for a development or change of use, the question of the nature of the locality will be determined by reference to the neighbourhood as it is with that development or change of use not as it was previously.

In *Gillingham BC v Medway (Chatham) Dock Co Ltd* (1993), the plaintiffs had granted planning permission for the change of a naval dockyard into a commercial dockyard, with the assurance given to the defendants that they would have unrestricted access to the dockyard and would be consulted before any change of access was made. Access to the dockyard was through a residential district and the plaintiffs sought an injunction to restrain the movement of lorries at night.

It was held that the question of the nature of the locality had to be determined by reference to the nature of the locality after the passing of the planning consents, not as it was previously.

Particular damage

The plaintiff must suffer direct and substantial damage to bring an action in public nuisance.

The following have been held to be special damage:

- Additional transport costs, caused by an obstruction: *Rose v Miles* (1815).

- Obstructing access to a coffee shop: *Benjamin v Storr* (1874).

- Obstructing the view of a procession so that the plaintiff lost profit on renting a room: *Campbell v Paddington BC* (1911).

The rule in Rylands v Fletcher

```
┌─────────────────────────────────────┐
│      Has there been an escape?       │
└─────────────────────────────────────┘
                  │
                  ▼
┌─────────────────────────────────────┐
│       Is there an accumulation?      │
└─────────────────────────────────────┘
                  │
                  ▼
┌─────────────────────────────────────┐
│  Is it something likely to do mischief? │
└─────────────────────────────────────┘
                  │
                  ▼
┌─────────────────────────────────────┐
│ Is it a 'non-natural' use of the land? │
└─────────────────────────────────────┘
                  │
                  ▼
┌─────────────────────────────────────┐
│     Is the damage foreseeable?       │
└─────────────────────────────────────┘
                  │
                  ▼
┌─────────────────────────────────────┐
│        Is there a defence?           │
└─────────────────────────────────────┘
```

The rule in *Rylands v Fletcher*

The rule in *Rylands v Fletcher* (1868) is a rule of strict liability, that is, it does not require proof of negligence or lack of care, or wrongful intention, on the part of the defendant. Actual damage must be proved, however; it is not a tort that is actionable *per se*.

The original statement

The rule was originally formulated by Blackburn J in *Rylands v Fletcher* in the following terms:

The person who for his own purposes brings on his land and collects and keeps there anything likely to do mischief if it escapes, must keep it in at his own peril and, if he does not do so, is *prima facie* answerable for all the damage which is the natural consequence of the escape.

This was approved by the House of Lords and the condition that there must be a 'non-natural user' was added by Lord Cairns.

Limits of the rule
These may be summarised as follows:

- There must have been an *escape* of something 'likely to do mischief'.

- There must have been a *non-natural use* of the land.

There must be an escape
In *Read v Lyons & Co Ltd* (1947), it was said that escape, for the purposes of applying the proposition in *Rylands v Fletcher*, means 'escape from a place where the defendant has occupation or control over land to a place which is outside his occupation or control', *per* Lord Simon, and 'there must be the escape of something from one man's close to another man's close', *per* Lord Macmillan.

In *Read v Lyons*, the plaintiff was a munitions worker who was injured by an exploding shell while in the defendant's munitions factory. It was held that there had not been an escape of a dangerous thing, so the defendant could not be liable under *Rylands v Fletcher*.

The plaintiff must prove not only that there has been an escape but that damage is a natural consequence of the escape.

Can a plaintiff sue for personal injuries?

There is some controversy as to what type of damage is recoverable under *Rylands v Fletcher*.

In *Read v Lyons*, it was questioned whether *Rylands v Fletcher* could be used for personal injuries claims, particularly by Lord Macmillan.

Nevertheless, it is now generally accepted that an occupier would be able to maintain an action for personal injuries.

In *Hale v Jennings* (1938), a 'chair-o-plane' from a fairground attraction became detached and landed on the plaintiff's stall on an adjoining ground. A claim for personal injuries was allowed. Such a claim was also allowed in *Miles v Forest Rock Granite Co Ltd* (1918).

In *Perry v Kendricks Transport* (1956), it was said that the plaintiff could recover for personal injuries even where he had no interest in the land affected.

However, the rule in *Rylands v Fletcher* will not extend so far as to cover situations whereby a plaintiff who has no interest in the land which is affected by the escape and whose only loss is financial: *Weller v Foot and Mouth DRI* (1966).

Does the plaintiff have to be an occupier?

There is a dispute as to whether or not it is necessary to have an interest in the land in order to maintain an action under the rule in *Rylands v Fletcher*.

While there are comments in such cases as *Read v Lyons* and *Weller v Foot and Mouth DRI* which seem to suggest that the plaintiff must be an occupier or have some interest in the land, there are other cases which adopt a broader view. Lawton J said *obiter* in *British Celanese v Hunt* (1969) that the plaintiff need not be the occupier of adjoining land, or any land. Furthermore, it was held that to use the premises for manufacturing was an ordinary use of the land.

The issue can only be settled by the House of Lords. An authoritative decision on this point is required.

Non-natural user

This requirement was added by Lord Cairns in the House of Lords in *Rylands v Fletcher* itself. This expression is highly flexible and enables the court to take into account their own interpretation of contemporaneous needs. The way the Privy Council expressed the position in *Rickards v Lothian* (1913) emphasised the flexibility:

> It must be some special use bringing with it increased danger to others and must not merely be the ordinary use of the land or such a use as is proper for the general benefit of the community.

There have, however, been decided cases which have maintained that certain circumstances can confidently be regarded as being outside the sphere of *Rylands v Fletcher* because the courts have held that the land is being naturally used. For example:

- lighting of a fire in a fire place: *Sochaki v Sas* (1947);

- storing metal foil strips in a factory: *British Celanese v Hunt* (1969).

In deciding what constitutes a natural use, Lord Porter in *Read v Lyons* said:

> … each seems to be a question of fact subject to a ruling by the judge as to whether … the particular use can be non-natural and in deciding this question I think that all the circumstances of the time and place

and practice of mankind must be taken into consideration, so what might be regarded as … non-natural may vary according to the circumstances.

For example, storage of motor parts and engines in *Mason v Levy Auto Parts* (1967) was not a natural use having regard to the large quantities of combustible material, manner of storage and character of the neighbourhood.

Non-natural use is a flexible concept and will vary according to time and context. For example, in *Perry v Kendricks Transport* (1956), the Court of Appeal found itself bound by the decision of *Musgrove v Pandelis* (1919) in holding that a full tank of petrol was a non-natural use of the land. Some commentators maintain that this would not be applied today.

Storage of chemicals for industrial use in large quantities was held to be a non-natural use in *Cambridge Water Co Ltd v Eastern Counties Leather plc* (1994).

In *Ellison v Ministry of Defence* (1997), rainwater which accumulated naturally on an airfield and not artificially kept there was held to be a natural use of the land. Consequently, it fell outside the rule in *Rylands v Fletcher*.

'Brings onto his land and keeps there'

The thing may or may not be something which in its nature is capable of being naturally there. What matters is whether the particular thing has in fact been accumulated there. *Rylands v Fletcher* only applies to things artificially brought or kept upon the defendant's land.

There is no liability for things naturally on the land, such as the spread of thistles from ploughed land in *Giles v Walker* (1890) or rocks falling from a natural outcrop in *Pontardawe RDC v Moore Gwyn* (1929).

More recently, flooding by rainwater was held to be something which occurred naturally on the land and was not an accumulation in *Ellison v Ministry of Defence* (1997).

These cases can be contrasted with *Crowhurst v Amersham Burial Board* (1878) where yew trees planted close to railings spread onto an adjoining meadow on which the plaintiff pastured his horse, which was poisoned and died as a result of eating yew leaves. The defendant was liable, although the yew trees were capable of being naturally there, the defendant had planted the trees and therefore they constituted an accumulation.

Liability in negligence and nuisance

The old common law rule was that an occupier was not under a duty to abate a nuisance that arises from his land as a result of natural causes. This was changed by the Privy Council in *Goldman v Hargrave* (1967) and was applied by the Court of Appeal in *Leakey v National Trust* (1980). The remedy for an escape of something occurring naturally on the land is, therefore, in nuisance or negligence not under *Rylands v Fletcher*.

'Anything likely to do mischief if it escapes'

This is a question of fact in each case. However, things which have been held to be within the rule include electricity, gas which was likely to pollute water supplies, explosives, fumes and water.

A very broad view can be taken. In *AG v Corke* (1933), it was held that the owner of land who allowed caravan dwellers to live on it was answerable for the interference they caused on adjoining land, on the basis that they were 'things likely to do mischief'.

Defences

Consent of the plaintiff

If the plaintiff has permitted the accumulation of the thing which escapes, then he cannot sue. Implied consent, such as common benefit, is also a defence.

Common benefit

If the accumulation benefits both the plaintiff and the defendant, this is an important element in deciding whether the plaintiff is deemed to have consented.

In *Carstairs v Taylor* (1871), rain water which had been collected on the roof of a block of flats for the benefit of several occupants meant that the landlord was not liable when the water escaped as it had been accumulated for a common benefit. In *Peters v Prince of Wales Theatre* (1943), a fire extinguisher which exploded damaging part of the building occupied by the plaintiffs was also held to have been accumulated for a common benefit.

Blackburn J spoke only of persons who 'for his own purposes' brings something onto his land. So, gas, water, electricity boards and inland waterways authorities carrying out statutory duties do not accumulate for their own purposes, so *Rylands v Fletcher* does not apply.

Act of a stranger
It is a defence that the escape was caused by the unforeseeable act of a stranger over whom the defendant has no control.

In *Rickards v Lothian* (1913), someone deliberately blocked a basin in the defendant's premises and turned the taps on, flooding the plaintiff's premises below. In *Perry v Kendricks Transport* (1956), the plaintiff was injured by an explosion caused by a boy trespasser who threw a lighted match into a petrol tank. The Court of Appeal held that the defendants were not liable as they had no control over trespassers and had not been negligent.

Foreseeable act of a stranger. The defendant in *Hale v Jennings* (1938) ought reasonably to have foreseen the act of a third party and had enough control over the premises to prevent the escape.

Act of God
If an escape is caused, through natural causes and without human intervention, in 'circumstances which no human foresight can provide against and of which human prudence is not bound to recognise the possibility', *Tennent v Earl of Glasgow* (1864), then there is said to be the defence of Act of God.

In *Nichols v Marsland* (1876), the defence succeeded where a violent thunderstorm caused flooding.

The case was put into proper perspective by the House of Lords in *Greenock Corporation v Caledonian Railway Company* (1917) where an extraordinary and unprecedented rainfall was held in similar circumstances not to be an Act of God. The explanation of *Nichols v Marsland* (1876) was that there the jury found that no reasonable person could have anticipated the storm and the court would not disturb a finding of fact.

Earthquakes and tornadoes may sometimes be Acts of God but few other phenomena seem likely to be within the scope of *Rylands v Fletcher*.

Statutory authority

Sometimes, public bodies storing water, gas, electricity and the like are by statute exempted from liability so long as they have taken reasonable care. It is a question of statutory interpretation whether, and, if so, to what extent, liability under *Rylands v Fletcher* is excluded.

Liability was excluded in *Green v Chelsea Waterworks Co* (1894) when, without negligence on the defendants' part, their water main exploded and flooded the plaintiff's premises.

This can be compared to *Charing Cross Electric Co v London Hydraulic Power Co* (1914) where the defendants were liable when their hydraulic main burst even though there was no question of negligence on their part, as the statute did not exempt them from liability.

Default of the plaintiff

The defendant is not liable where damage is cause by the plaintiff's act or default. If the plaintiff is partially responsible, then the Law Reform (Contributory Negligence) Act 1945 will apply.

In *Ponting v Noakes* (1894), the defendant's colt reached over the defendant's land and ate some branches of a yew tree and died. The action did not succeed as the animal's death was due to its wrongful intrusion.

Where the damage is attributable to the extra sensitivity of the plaintiff's property, then there is no liability: *Eastern and South African Telegraph Co Ltd v Cape Town Tramways Co Ltd* (1902).

Remoteness of damage

Negligence	Private nuisance	*Rylands v Fletcher*
Reasonable foreseeability: *The Wagon Mound (No 1)* but also competing test of direct consequences: *Re Polemis* (1921) *Page v Smith*	Reasonable foreseeability: *Wagon Mound (No 2)* (1967)	Reasonable foreseeability: *Cambridge Water v Eastern Counties Leather* (1994)

Blackburn J said that a defendant is *prima facie* liable for all the damage which is the natural consequence of the escape.

It was argued that, following the decision of the Privy Council in *The Wagon Mound (No 2)* (1967), if the test for remoteness of damage is foreseeability, then the test in *Rylands v Fletcher* is also foreseeability.

It has also been argued that where damage has been caused as a result of the extraordinary risk created by the defendant then the defendant should be liable for the unforeseeable risk.

An important development has been the House of Lords decision in *Cambridge Water Co Ltd v Eastern Counties Leather plc* (1994). It was held that foreseeability of damage was an essential prerequisite of liability. Strict liability arises only if the defendant knows or ought to foresee that the thing which is stored might cause damage if it escapes. Once there is such knowledge or foreseeability, the defendant is liable even if he takes all reasonable care to prevent the escape.

Future of strict liability for hazardous activities

The scope of the rule in *Rylands v Fletcher* has been cut down considerably by the requirements that there be a non-natural use and the exclusion of 'ordinary' industrial processes: *British Celanese v Hunt* (1969).

The defences, particularly act of a stranger and statutory authority, turn a tort of strict liability into an inquisition on the defendant's culpability.

The Pearson Commission recommended a statutory scheme of strict liability for personal injuries resulting from exceptional risks. Under the scheme, strict liability would be imposed in two circumstances:

- those which by their unusually hazardous activities require close, careful supervision; and

- those which, although normally safe, are likely to cause serious and extensive casualties if they do go wrong.

Contributory negligence and voluntary assumption of the risk would be general defences but statutory authority and act of a third party would not. The fact that the plaintiff was a trespasser would not be a general defence but could be introduced as a defence to a specific type of exceptional risk when making the statutory instrument.

4 General defences

So far, we have been primarily concerned with what a plaintiff has to prove in order to establish the existence of a tort.

This would be a convenient point to consider certain defences which may be raised by the defendant who, while admitting the behaviour complained of (which would otherwise constitute a tort), then seeks to adduce in evidence additional facts which will excuse what he has done. So, the burden of proving the facts to establish the defence rests on the defendant.

Contributory negligence

Position at common law
At common law, it was a complete defence if the defendant proved that the plaintiff had been guilty of contributory negligence. In *Butterfield v Forrester* (1809), the defendant negligently left a pole lying across the road. The plaintiff was injured when he collided with the pole when riding along the road. Although the defendant had been negligent he escaped liability, as the plaintiff would have avoided the accident if he had not been riding so fast.

Last opportunity. This resulted in undue hardship to the plaintiff and so to mitigate its harshness the courts' developed the rule of 'last opportunity' which meant that whoever was negligent last in time was treated as the sole cause of the damage on the basis that they had been the last one to have the opportunity to avoid the accident. The rule was applied in *Davies v Mann* (1842). The plaintiff tied the feet of his donkey and negligently left him on the highway.

The defendant who was driving his wagon faster than necessary collided with the donkey, which was killed. The defendant was liable. If he had been driving at the correct speed, he would have avoided the donkey, so he had the last opportunity to avoid the accident.

A rule of 'constructive last opportunity' was created in *British Columbia Electric Railway Co Ltd v Loach* (1916).

Law Reform (Contributory Negligence) Act 1945
This linear sequential approach to liability was most difficult to apply in cases where events occurred simultaneously.

The problems led to the Law Reform (Contributory Negligence) Act 1945, which introduced apportionment of damages for accidents occurring on land. It is now possible for the courts to reduce the damages awarded against the defendant to the extent to which the plaintiff was contributorily negligent. It was held by the Court of Appeal in *Pitts v Hunt* (1991) that damages can never be reduced by 100% and therefore contributory negligence can only be a partial defence.

Scope of the Law Reform (Contributory Negligence) Act 1945
Under s 4 of the Act, fault means 'negligence, breach of statutory duty or other act or omission which gives rise to liability in tort'. So the Act applies to nuisance and *Rylands v Fletcher* as well as negligence.

In order to establish and prove contributory negligence, the defendant must plead and prove:

- that the plaintiff's injury results from the risk which the plaintiff's negligence exposed him;

- that the plaintiff's negligence contributed to his injury;

- that there was fault or negligence on the part of the plaintiff.

Plaintiff's negligence contributed to his injury

It is not necessary to show that the plaintiff owes the defendant a duty of care, merely that the plaintiff has contributed to the injury and not necessarily the cause of the accident. So, in *O'Connell v Jackson* (1972), there was a 15% reduction in the damages awarded to a motor-cyclist because of his failure to wear a crash helmet. Similarly, in *Froom v Butcher* (1976), there was a 25% reduction to a driver for failure to wear a seatbelt, as the injury could have been completely avoided by wearing the seat belt, but if wearing a seat belt would have reduced the severity of the injuries, then damages would have been reduced by 15%.

Other examples of the plaintiff having contributed to the injury include the failure of a motor cyclist to fasten the chin strap of a crash helmet: *Capps v Miller* (1989); accepting a lift in a car knowing that the driver is drunk: *Owens v Brimmell* (1977), although the burden is on the defendant to show that the plaintiff knew that the defendant was unfit to drive: *Limbrick v French* (1993); asking a much younger inexperienced driver to drive a car when the driver has never driven a powerful, automatic car before: *Donelan v Donelan* (1993) and crossing a pelican crossing when the pedestrian light is red: *Fitzgerald v Lane* (1989). In *Commissioner of Police for the Metropolis v Reeves* (1999), the House of Lords held that a prisoner who hanged himself in police custody had been contributorily negligent in relation to his own death.

Plaintiff's injury results from the risk which he exposed himself

In *Jones v Livox Quarries Ltd* (1952), the plaintiff was riding on the back of the defendant's vehicle contrary to instructions. A vehicle collided into the back, injuring the plaintiff. He argued, unsuccessfully, that he had exposed himself to the risk of falling off not to a collision.

The standard of care

This is the same standard of care as that in negligence:

> A person is guilty of contributory negligence if he ought reasonably to have foreseen that, if he did not act as a reasonable, prudent man, he might hurt himself and in his reckonings he must take into account the possibility of others being careless (*per* Lord Denning in *Jones v Livox Quarries*).

In practice, though, the courts seem to demand less of plaintiffs than defendants.

A look at some particular instances:

(1) Children

Denning LJ in *Gough v Thorne* (1966) said that a very young child could not be contributorily negligent.

However, the general test seems to be: what degree of care can an infant of a particular age reasonably be expected to take for his own safety (*Yachuk v Oliver Blais Co Ltd* (1949))? Consequently, a 12 year old girl was contributorily negligent in *Armstrong v Cotterell* (1993), as a child of that age is expected to know the basic elements of the Highway Code.

In *J v West* (1999), the Court of Appeal held that a nine year old, who had jumped off a kerb into the path of a car to avoid being hit by a friend, was not contributorily negligent.

It was held in *Oliver v Birmingham and Midland Omnibus Co Ltd* (1933) that, where a child is under the control of an adult, negligence on the part of the adult is not imputed to the child.

(2) Accidents at work

The purpose of such statutory regulations as the Factories Acts and those made under the Health and Safety at Work, etc, Act 1974 is to ensure safety standards in workplaces and to protect workers from their own carelessness.

This being the purpose behind such regulations, in order to ensure that their purpose is not defeated by finding contributory negligence, the courts tend to be less willing to make a finding of contributory negligence in these cases. See *Caswell v Powell Duffryn Associated Collieries Ltd* (1940).

This does not mean that a workman can never be guilty of contributory negligence. In *Jayes v IMI (Kynoch) Ltd* (1985), a workman who put his hand into a piece of moving machinery had his damages reduced by 100%, even though the employer was in breach of his statutory duty to fence the machinery. It should be noted that this case was heard prior to *Pitts v Hunt* (1991) and damages can now never be reduced by 100%.

(3) Emergency

An emergency is a special situation in which a person's reactions may with hindsight be regarded as negligent. The law takes account of this and provided the defendant has acted reasonably he will not be held to have been contributorily negligent. See *Jones v Boyce* (1816).

Consent/*volenti non fit injuria*

There is considerable confusion between these two concepts. Consent is used to describe the defence that may be used when sued for committing an intentional tort.

Volenti non fit injuria is the appropriate term where the plaintiff alleges negligence/strict liability tort, that is, an unintentional tort, which claims the defendant's voluntary assumption of the risk involved.

However, the general principles applying to both concepts are the same but it is important to bear in mind the stature of the tort concerned.

The defence of consent was found to be available to a defendant who clamped the plaintiff's car in *Arthur v Anker* (1995). However, certain conditions had to be satisfied before the defence would arise. There would have to be a notice that a vehicle parked without lawful authority would be clamped and released on payment of a fee. The release fee would have to be reasonable. The vehicle would have to be released without delay, once the owner had offered to pay and there would have to be means by which the owner could communicate his offer of payment.

Mere knowledge does not imply consent

In the case of *Smith v Baker & Sons* (1891), the plaintiff was an employee of the defendants and was employed in drilling holes in rock cutting and was aware of the danger of a crane continually swinging over his head. A stone fell out of the crane and injured him. He brought an action in negligence and *volenti non fit injuria* was pleaded.

It was held that mere knowledge of the risk was not enough, it had to be shown that the plaintiff had consented to the particular thing being done which would involve the risk and consented to take that risk upon himself.

The question in *Dann v Hamilton* (1939) was whether a plaintiff who accepted a lift from a drunk driver who was obviously inebriated could be taken to have assumed the risk of injury. It was held that *volenti* did not apply, unless the drunkenness was so extreme and so glaring that accepting lift was equivalent to 'walking on the edge of an unfenced cliff'.

Under s 149 of the Road Traffic Act 1988, defendants are prevented from relying on the *volenti* defence where a passenger sues a driver in circumstances where, under the Act, insurance is compulsory.

It does not apply where there is no requirement of compulsory insurance under the Act, for example, an aeroplane. In *Morris v Murray* (1991), two men involved in a drinking session took a plane on a flight. The plane crashed but the plaintiff passenger was held to be *volens* as he must have known the state the pilot was in.

To be effective consent must be freely given

Normally, as already shown in *Smith v Baker & Sons*, an employee will rarely be held to be *volenti* but there are exceptional cases, such as *ICI v Shatwell* (1965). The plaintiff and his brother disregarded the instructions of their employer and were also in breach of statutory safety regulations and chose to test certain detonators without seeking the necessary precautions. The plaintiff was injured in the subsequent explosion. The plaintiff's action in both negligence and breach of statutory duty failed because of *volenti non fit injuria*. This is an unusual case, however, and *volenti* will not normally arise out of an employee's ordinary duties.

Rescue cases

The law is reluctant to apply *volenti* to rescue situations, because to do so would negative the duty of care owed to the plaintiff.

In *Haynes v Harwood* (1935), a two-horse van was left unattended in the street. A boy threw a stone and the horses ran off and were threatening a woman and children. A policeman intercepted and stopped the horses and was injured. It was held that the *volenti* defence did not apply. *Volenti* will apply where there is no real risk of danger and there is not a genuine emergency: *Cutler v United Dairies (London) Ltd* (1933).

Sporting events

In *Smolden v Whitworth* (1997), a colts rugby player sued the referee in negligence for failing to control the scrum properly. The plaintiff suffered a broken back when the scrum collapsed. It was held that the player had consented to the ordinary incidents of the game. He cannot be said to have consented to the breach of duty of an official whose job was to enforce the rules.

In *McCord v Swansea City AFC* (1997), it was held that recklessness was not required to be shown after a clear foul which was outside the laws of the game as there is no *volens* to such acts.

Illegal acts

A person who is engaged in an illegal act at the time he is injured may be precluded from a civil claim by the maxim *'ex turpi causa non oritur actio'* (bad people get less).

A distinction was made by Asquith LJ in *National Coal Board v England* (1954) between two different types of situation:

- the case of two burglars on their way to commit a burglary and while proceeding one picks the other's pocket; and

- where they have agreed to open a safe by means of high explosive and one negligently handles the explosive charge injuring the other.

In the first situation, Asquith LJ thought that there would be liability in tort but not in the second. The idea being where the illegality is incidental to the cause of action in tort then recovery in tort may still be allowed.

It was held in *Ashton v Turner* (1981) that one participant in a burglary could not succeed against his fellow participant who crashed the car while driving away at high speed from the scene of the crime.

In the case of *Pitts v Hunt* (1991), the plaintiff was a pillion passenger on a motorcycle. Both the plaintiff and the defendant who was riding the motorcycle were drunk. The plaintiff also knew that the defendant was unlicensed and uninsured. The defendant carelessly crashed the motorcycle, killing himself and injuring the plaintiff. Due to s 149 Road Traffic Act 1988, the defence of *volenti* did not apply. Nevertheless, the plaintiff was found to be *ex turpi*. The majority of the Court of Appeal held that because of the joint illegal activity it was impossible to determine the standard of care.

Most cases have not followed this standard of care test but have, instead, used a test based on whether it would be an affront to public conscience to compensate the plaintiff.

In *Revill v Newberry* (1995), it was held that the rule did not apply in a claim for personal injuries where the plaintiff was a trespasser engaged in criminal activities and the defendant had shot the plaintiff. The defendant was found to have acted negligently and to have denied the plaintiff, who had been contributorily negligent, any compensation would have effectively made him an outlaw. The case was distinguished from a 'joint criminal enterprise', such as *Pitts v Hunt*. Evans LJ held that it is one thing to deny a plaintiff any fruits from his illegal conduct but different, and more far reaching, to deprive him of compensation for injury which he had suffered and which was otherwise entitled to recover at law.

The defence of illegality was invoked on grounds of public policy in *Clunis v Camden and Islington Health Authority* (1998). The plaintiff who suffered from a mental illness attacked and killed a stranger. He sued his health authority in negligence, as they had released him prematurely.

Immoral conduct
Ex turpi applies not only to criminal conduct but can also apply to immoral conduct, as well. In *Kirkham v Chief Constable of the Greater Manchester Police* (1990), it was said that suicide committed by someone 'wholly sane' would be *ex turpi* but, in that particular case, it did not apply as there was grave mental instability.

Mistake

Mistake as to law or to fact is not a general defence. Mistake is not a defence to an intentional tort such as trespass or conversion, however, unreasonable.

Inevitable accident

This used to be a defence in trespass but now liability in trespass depends upon proof of intention.

Whereas, in negligence, if it can be shown that the accident could not have been avoided by the exercise of reasonable care, then that amounts to a claim that the behaviour was not negligent.

Statutory authority

A statute may authorise what would otherwise be a tort and an injured party will have no remedy save for that provided by statute.

Statutes often confer powers to act on public and other authorities. Such power will not in general be a defence to a claim in tort.

Limitation of actions

In actions at common law, there is no limitation period. The rules on limitation are entirely statutory and are now contained in the Limitation Act 1980.

The basic rule is that an action cannot be brought more than six years from the date the cause of action accrued: s 2 of the Limitation Act 1980.

There are four situations in which different rules apply:

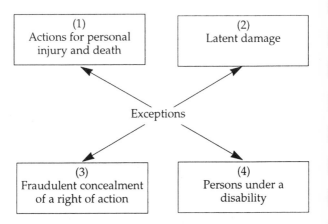

| (1) Actions for personal injury and death | (2) Latent damage |

Exceptions

| (3) Fraudulent concealment of a right of action | (4) Persons under a disability |

(1) Actions for personal injury and death

In actions for personal injuries, the basic limitation period is three years from either the date on which the cause of action accrued or the date of the plaintiff's knowledge whichever is the later: s 11(4) of the Limitation Act 1980. The court has a wide discretion to disregard this time limit and permit the action to proceed by virtue of s 33 of the Limitation Act 1980.

However, s 11 does not apply to permit the exercise of the discretion in cases of deliberately inflicted injury such as child abuse: *Stubbings v Webb* (1992) (HL).

The cause of action accrues when the plaintiff suffers actionable damage irrespective of the plaintiff's knowledge of the damage: *Cartledge v E Jobling & Sons Ltd* (1963).

But, the 'date of knowledge' is defined in s 15 of the Limitation Act 1980. The plaintiff has knowledge of the cause of action when he first has knowledge of the following facts:

- that the injury was significant; and

- that the injury was attributable in whole or in part to the act or omission which is alleged to constitute negligence, nuisance or breach of duty; and

- the identity of the defendant; and

- if it is alleged that the act or omission was that of a person other than the defendant, the identity of that person and the additional facts supporting the bringing of an action against the defendant.

An injury is 'significant' if it would justify proceedings against a defendant who did not dispute liability and was able to satisfy the judgment. Knowledge includes 'constructive knowledge', that is, knowledge a person might reasonably have been expected to acquire.

After a major operation, the date of knowledge for the purposes of s 11 of the Limitation Act 1980 occurs as soon as the plaintiff has had time to overcome the shock of the injury, take stock of his disability and seek advice (*Forbes v Wandsworth HA* (1996)).

With regard to the discretion given by s 33, the court will have regard to all the circumstances and the exercise of the discretion is something of a lottery. The discretion was held to be unfettered in *Firman v Ellis* (1978).

By s 33(3), the court must have regard to particular aspects of the matter: for example, the length and reasons for the delay; the defendant's conduct; the effect of delay on the evidence; the plaintiff's conduct, etc.

In deciding whether to exercise its discretion whether to disapply the three year rule under s 33 of the Limitation Act, the court should apply a subjective rather than an objective test as to the reasons for the plaintiff's delay in instituting proceedings (*Coad v Cornwall and Isles of Scilly HA* (1996)).

A subjective test was again applied in *Spargo v North Essex District Health Authority* (1997).

(2) Latent damage

Where damage is latent, the plaintiff will be unaware that the damage has actually occurred. As a result, the cause of action may accrue and become statute barred before the plaintiff even knows about the damage or his right to sue.

In *Cartledge v E Jobling & Sons Ltd* (1963), the plaintiff contracted pneumoconiosis from the inhalation of dust over a long period of working in a particular environment. The damage to the lungs was latent and the plaintiff was unaware of it.

The House of Lords held that the cause of action accrued when significant damage to the lungs occurred and it was irrelevant that the plaintiff knew of the damage or not. As a result of this decision, the law of limitation was changed by statute in relation to personal injuries.

This left the problem of what to do about defective buildings. Various tests for the commencement of the limitation period were developed. For example:

- some felt the limitation period should begin with the date of construction;

- others felt that time should run when the plaintiff discovered the damage or ought reasonably to have done so.

However, the case of *Pirelli General Cable Works Ltd v Oscar Faber & Partners* (1983) held that the action accrued and, therefore, the limitation period commenced when physical damage to the building actually occurred, regardless of whether it could be discovered by the plaintiff. A distinction is made between structural fault and the defect arising from it. The *Pirelli* case maintains that the action accrues at the time the physical damage occurs.

Pirelli has caused one or two problems. The Latent Damage Act 1986 tries to redress the problem. It introduced a special extension of the limitation period in respect of latent damage (other than physical injury) and it gives the plaintiff three years from the date on which he discovered significant damage. This amends the Limitation Act accordingly. All claims are subject to an absolute bar for claims for 15 years from the date of the defendant's negligence.

The 1986 Act is an attempt to redress the balance between the plaintiff and the defendant in latent or postponed damage cases.

All this has been overtaken by *Murphy v Brentwood DC* (1990) where it was held that damage for a latent defect in a building itself is not recoverable in negligence as it is pure economic loss.

(3) Fraudulent concealment of a right of action
Where the defendant has deliberately concealed from the plaintiff the facts of a tort the period of limitation does not commence until the plaintiff has discovered the fraud or could with reasonable diligence have done so.

Therefore, in *Kitchen v Royal Air Force Association* (1958), a failure by solicitors to inform the plaintiff of an offer of £100 by potential defendants because that might reveal their own negligence at an earlier stage, constituted deliberate concealment.

(4) Persons under a disability

Time does not run against an infant, or a person of unsound mind, until he ceases to be under a disability or dies, whichever occurs.

However, if the plaintiff was not under a disability when the action accrued but subsequently becomes of unsound mind this will not prevent time from running.

5 Remedies

In considering remedies, it should be remembered that tort compensation is not the principal form of compensation. The plaintiff's chances of receiving adequate compensation will depend on whether he can prove the defendant was at fault and whether the defendant has adequate resources to compensate the plaintiff. The tort system interlinks with other compensation systems. It is no coincidence that a high proportion of tort damages are in respect of road accidents, industrial accidents and medical mishaps. The insurance system works behind the scenes to ensure that the plaintiff is adequately compensated in these types of cases. There is also an interaction between the tort system and other forms of compensation such as social security, criminal injuries compensation and workers' compensation.

Aims of compensation

The aim of tort compensation is to restore the plaintiff to the position he would have been in had the tort not been committed: *Livingstone v Rawyards Coal Co* (1880).

It has been argued that the compensation system is based on the wrong principles. The plaintiff is compensated for what he has actually lost. The defendant is therefore liable for a greater amount of damages if he injures a high earning plaintiff as opposed to a low earning plaintiff. It has been said that damages should be based on what plaintiff needs rather than on what he has lost. This is particularly relevant in cases of severe injury.

Further criticisms are based on the guesswork involved in calculating future loss and that compensation depends on the fault principle. Both of these points are considered in greater depth below.

A single action and lump sum

A plaintiff can only bring one action in respect of a single wrong. He cannot maintain a second action based on the same facts merely because the damage turns out to be more extensive than was anticipated. He can recover damages once only and the cause of the action is extinguished by the action. The authority for this is *Fetter v Beale* (1701) where a plaintiff failed in his claim for further damages after his medical condition deteriorated following his first award of damages.

But, if one and the same act violates two rights which are accorded separate protection by the law of torts, then there are two separate causes of action, the prosecution of one of which will not bar proceedings in respect of the other.

In *Brunsden v Humphrey* (1884), a cab driven by the plaintiff collided with the defendant's van through the negligent driving of the defendant's servant. In county court proceedings, the plaintiff recovered compensation for damage to his cab. He then brought a second action in the High Court for personal injuries sustained by him in the same collision and the Court of Appeal held that this action was not barred by an earlier one.

Damages are assessed once and for all and can be awarded in the form of a lump sum or, since 1989, it has been possible to receive a structured settlement, whereby the damages are divided into a lump sum and periodic payments. This principle causes difficulties where loss in the future is uncertain. In personal injury actions, the plaintiff's medical condition may become much worse or much better than expected. In the words of Lord Scarman in *Lim Poh Choo v Camden and Islington AHA* (1980):

> Knowledge of the future being denied to mankind, so much of the award as is attributed to future loss and suffering will almost surely be wrong. There is only one certainty: the future will prove the award to be either too high or too low.

Disadvantages of lump sum system

A number of criticisms have been made of the lump sum system. These can be identified, as follows:

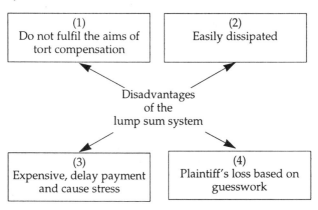

(1) Lump sums do not fulfil the aims of tort compensation

The aim of tort damages is to place the defendant in the position he would have been in if the tort had not been committed. A lump sum carries with it the responsibility of investment, to ensure future income from the lump sum. If the plaintiff was to be truly compensated for his loss, then he would receive a regular income in place of his lost earnings.

(2) Lump sums are easily dissipated

There is nothing preventing the plaintiff from spending the lump sum before the end of the period for which it was intended that the plaintiff would be compensated. This would leave the plaintiff making a claim against the Welfare State and be doubly compensated for a single injury.

(3) Lump sums are expensive, delay payment and cause stress

As lump sums are a once and for all system of compensation, they tend to encourage delay prior to settlement. There is every incentive to wait until the plaintiff's condition has stabilised, as much as possible, to ensure that the *quantum* of damages reflects the plaintiff's loss as closely as possible. Because an assessment of the plaintiff's future condition involves guesswork, reliance is placed on expert reports, which frequently conflict and this increases delay and costs. There is little incentive for the defendant to settle early. The plaintiff may be in receipt of welfare payments which may pressurise him into settling early and for too little. A medical condition termed 'compensation neurosis' has been identified, whereby the plaintiff's condition fails to improve pending the outcome of the case. In addition, once the case has been settled the plaintiff has to manage a sum which is probably greater than any other he has had to deal with in his life and also ensure that it lasts for the rest of his life.

(4) Lump sums are based on guesswork

A number of projections have to be made when assessing the plaintiff's loss under the lump sum system. His future condition, his future earning prospects, his promotion prospects prior to the accident, etc. A lump sum system does not allow for a change in circumstance, whereas a system of periodic payments can allow for occasional review.

Types of damage

Nominal damages

Nominal damages are awarded where the plaintiff has proved his case but has suffered no loss: *Constantine v Imperial Hotels Ltd* (1944). The plaintiff will only be awarded a small amount of money. Nominal damage can only be awarded for those torts which are actionable *per se*.

Contemptuous damages

Contemptuous damages are awarded where the action is technically successful but is without merit and the action should not have been brought. The amount of damages is usually the smallest coin in the realm. The judge will normally order the plaintiff to pay his own costs and may even order him to pay the defendant's costs as well.

Aggravated damages

Aggravated damages are compensatory. They are awarded where the plaintiff has suffered more than can reasonably be expected in the situation. They will be awarded where the plaintiff's proper feelings of dignity and pride have been injured: *Jolliffe v Willmett & Co* (1971). They have also been awarded where the tort was committed in a malicious, insulting or oppressive manner: *Broome v Cassell & Co Ltd* (1972). They will not be awarded in cases of personal injury where the tort was committed in a way that was more painful than necessary, as a higher award for pain and suffering will reflect this: *Kralj v McGrath* (1986); *AB v South West Water Services Ltd* (1993).

The Law Commission in its 1997 report, *Aggravated, Exemplary and Restitutionary Damages*, recommended that aggravated damages should be re-named 'damages for mental distress' to make it clear that they are compensatory.

Exemplary damages

Exemplary damages are intended to be punitive and can therefore be distinguished from aggravated damages which are compensatory. They take the form of an additional award on top of the compensatory award. They are an exception to the rule that the aim of damages in tort is to compensate. They are unpopular with judges as exemplary damages confuse the aims of the criminal and civil law and it is also thought undesirable to punish a defendant without the safeguards inherent in the criminal law. By contrast, it has been argued, most notably by Lord Wilberforce in *Broome v Cassell & Co Ltd* (1972), that tort has a deterrent function in addition to a compensatory function and that exemplary damages are therefore a legitimate part of the compensation system. Nevertheless, a restrictive approach has been taken and it was held in *Rookes v Barnard* (1964) that exemplary damages could only be awarded in three situations.

• Oppressive, arbitrary or unconstitutional action by servants of government. The term 'servants of the government' includes police officers and also local and central government officials. It was held in *AB v South West Water Services Ltd* (1993) that publicly owned utilities which provide a monopoly service are outside the category.

A man who had been seriously assaulted by police officers was entitled to substantial exemplary damages and these damages were not reduced on the grounds of his serious previous convictions in *Treadaway v Chief Constable of West Midlands* (1994).

- Where the defendant's conduct has been calculated to make a profit for himself which exceeds the compensation payable. In *Broome v Cassell & Co Ltd* (1972), the defendants published a book which the knew contained defamatory statements about the plaintiff. They believed that the increased profits from the sale would exceed any award of damages. £15,000 compensatory damages were awarded and an additional £25,000 exemplary damages. In *AB v South West Water Services Ltd* (1993), covering up the existence of a tort did not come within this category.

- Where statute authorises the award of exemplary damages. In *AB v South West Water Services Ltd* (1993), it was held by the Court of Appeal that exemplary damages could not be awarded in negligence, deceit, breach of statutory duty or public nuisance. The court's reasoning was based on *Rookes v Barnard* (1964). The House of Lords had attempted to limit exemplary damages in that case; thus it is not possible to award such damages unless they were available for that type of tort prior to 1964.

The Court of Appeal laid down guidelines to juries for the award of exemplary damages against the police in *Thompson v Commissioner of Police of the Metropolis* (1997). It is unlikely to be less than £5,000 and might be as much as £25,000 where an officer of the rank of superintendent or above is involved.

The Law Commission in its 1997 report, *Aggravated, Exemplary and Restitutionary Damages*, recommended that exemplary damages be re-named 'punitive damages'. A judge, as opposed to a jury, should recommend whether they are awardable and their amount. Defendants should be liable to pay them for any tort or equitable wrong or a civil wrong arising under statute in any case where the defendant's behaviour in committing the wrong or after it has been committed deliberately or outrageously disregarded the plaintiff's rights.

General and special damages

There are two meanings to these terms. First, general damages can mean the damage that is presumed to flow from torts which are actionable *per se,* for example, trespass, and special damage is the damage the plaintiff must prove where damage is an element of the tort, for example, negligence.

The second and most common meaning is that general damages are those which cannot be calculated precisely, whereas special damages are those which can be calculated precisely at the date of trial.

Damages in personal injury actions

A plaintiff who suffers injuries incurs two types of loss. Pecuniary loss, for example, loss of earnings, expenses, etc and non-pecuniary loss for example, pain and suffering, loss of a limb.

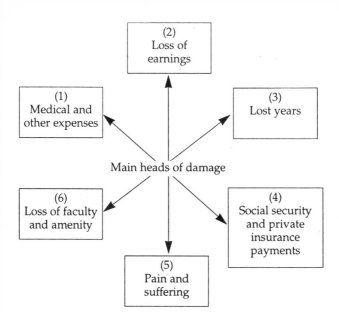

```
                    (2)
                 Loss of
                 earnings


  (1)                                   (3)
Medical and                          Lost years
other expenses

              Main heads of damage


  (6)                                   (4)
Loss of faculty                      Social security
and amenity                          and private
                                     insurance
                    (5)              payments
                 Pain and
                 suffering
```

(1) Medical and other expenses

Under s 2(4) of the Law Reform (Personal Injuries) Act 1948, the plaintiff may incur private medical expenses and recover the same, despite the availability of the NHS. The Pearson Commission recommended that private medical expenses should only be recoverable where it was reasonable that they should be incurred on medical grounds but this proposal has not been implemented.

Section 5 Administration of Justice Act 1982 provides that where an injured person makes a saving by being maintained at public expense in a hospital, nursing home or other institution, then these savings must be set off against his loss of income. The Road Traffic (NHS Charges) Act 1999 enables NHS Hospitals to recover the cost of treating accident victims from defendants' insurers.

If the plaintiff has to change to special accommodation as a result of his injuries, then the additional annual cost over ordinary accommodation is recoverable. The cost of adapting accommodation or a car to special needs is also recoverable. The capital cost of special accommodation or car is not recoverable as it is an asset which belongs to the plaintiff.

An example of an additional expense incurred as a result of a tort is contained in *Jones v Jones* (1985). The plaintiff's injuries led to the breakdown of his marriage. The Court of Appeal held that the extra cost to the plaintiff of having to finance two homes instead of one was, in principle, recoverable. This case has been criticised on the basis that it is not felt that marriage breakdown is really foreseeable. By contrast, it was held in *Pritchard v JH Cobden Ltd* (1988) that the cost of a marriage breakdown caused by injuries were not recoverable either because it was too remote or on grounds that it was contrary to public policy.

In *Donelly v Joyce* (1974), the plaintiff's loss included the cost incurred by a third party. For example, where a relative or friend provides nursing assistance or financial assistance, then this can be catered for in the plaintiff's claim. Where a relative has given up work, then the loss of earnings will be recoverable provided they do not exceed the commercial cost of nursing care: *Housecroft v Burnett* (1986).

(2) Loss of earnings

This can be divided into:

- actual loss;

- future loss.

Actual loss runs from the date of the accident to the date of assessment (settlement or trial). It is not permissible to profit from loss of earnings, so income tax and social security contributions must be deducted in order to ascertain the net loss: *British Transport Commission v Gourley* (1956). Loss of perquisites, for example, a company car are also taken into account.

Future loss is speculative and relates to losses the plaintiff will suffer after the date of assessment.

First, it is necessary to calculate the net loss of earnings, this is known as the multipicand. Tax and social security contributions are deducted from the plaintiff's earnings to arrive at the net figure. The multiplicand is adjusted to take account of future promotion prospects.

The multiplicand is multiplied by an appropriate multiplier up to a maximum of 18. In practice, the multiplier is rarely this high as it is discounted to take account of future uncertainties and also accelerated receipt. A return on capital invested is taken as 4½% and the sum awarded which is invested should provide for lost earnings, the plaintiff being expected to live off the investment income and part of the capital. Future inflation is not taken into account as that should be covered by shrewd investment. In cases of very large awards, the House of Lords held in *Hodgson v Trapp* (1988) that the multiplier could not be increased to reflect the fact that the plaintiff would be paying tax at higher tax levels.

There has been a flurry of recent case law concerning the multiplier. At first instance, in *Wells v Wells* (1995); *Thomas v Brighton Health Authority* (1995) and *Page v Sheerness Steel Co plc* (1995), the judge fixed the multiplier by reference to the return on index linked government securities at 3% a year. These are safe investments, involving minimum risk. The effect was to make the multiplier significantly higher and the damages were greatly increased.

All three cases were heard together in the Court of Appeal in 1996 where it was held that the assumption in large awards was that the plaintiff would seek advice on how to manage the money. A basket of investment would include a substantial proportion of riskier equities as well as index-linked government securities. Consequently, the conventional discount rate of 4.5% continued to apply.

When the joined appeals reached the House of Lords in 1998, it was accepted that it must be assumed that investment will be based on Index Linked Government Securities (ILGS). However, a prudent investment would be based on a balanced portfolio which would include some riskier equities. The House of Lords held that the rate of return (and hence discount) should be based on ILGS giving an average return of 3%. Consequently, the awards in the cases were raised. It is believed that this decision has been responsible for a series of very high awards of damages after July 1998 in cases involving long term future care.

(3) 'Lost years'

Where the plaintiff's life expectancy has been reduced as a result of his injuries, the question whether the plaintiff can be compensated for the earnings he would have received between the date of his expected death and the date he would have stopped working if it hadn't have been for the accident.

It was held in *Oliver v Ashman* (1962) that claims for the lost years were not recoverable.

The House of Lords overruled *Oliver v Ashman* in *Pickett v British Rail Engineering* (1980) and damages for prospective loss of earnings are now awarded for the whole of the plaintiff's pre-accident life expectancy, subject to deduction of the plaintiff's living expenses.

(4) Social security and private insurance payments

Some social security payments are deducted from the plaintiff's loss of income. Section 22 of the Social Security Act 1989 which is now incorporated into the Social Security Administration Act 1992 enables welfare payments made to the plaintiff to be recouped from the defendant. The system was amended by the Social Security (Recovery of Benefits) Act 1997. The full value of all recoverable benefits during the relevant period (applying to all settlements and judgments after 6 October 1997) must be deducted before payment from the plaintiff's damages. The defendant cannot pay the damages award until he has obtained a certificate of the benefits paid or payable and recovered the same from the award.

Private insurance payments are not deducted as the defendant would therefore profit from the plaintiff's foresight. Payments made under an accident insurance policy taken out by an employer on behalf of employees is also non deductible: *McCamley v Cammell Laird Shipbuilders Ltd* (1990). *Ex gratia* payments made by a charity are also not deductible. An occupational disability pension is not deducted: *Parry v Cleaver* (1970). This was affirmed in

Smoker v London Fire and Civil Defence Authority (1991) on the basis that a pension is deferred payment. Occupational sick pay will be deducted: *Hussain v New Taplow Paper Mills Ltd* (1988).

In *Longdon v British Coal Corporation* (1998), the House of Lords held that an incapacity pension awarded before normal retirement age should not be deducted.

(5) Pain and suffering

The plaintiff is entitled to be compensated for actual and prospective pain and suffering. Section 1(1)(b) of the Administration of Justice Act 1982 allows a plaintiff who knows that his life expectancy has been reduced to recover for that anguish. A permanently unconscious plaintiff cannot claim for pain and suffering: *Wise v Kaye* (1962).

(6) Loss of faculty and amenity

A tariff system of £X for the loss of a leg and £Y for the loss of an arm exists. Refer to *Kemp and Kemp* for details. Loss of amenity involves the lost chances to use the faculty. Loss of amenity will be greater for a keen sportsman that loses a leg than a couch potato who spends his life watching TV.

The award of loss of amenity is made objectively, see, for example, *H West & Sons Ltd v Shephard* (1964) where the plaintiff was unconscious and unable to appreciate his condition.

New methods of paying damages in personal injury cases

Structured settlements

For many years, damages were assessed once and paid in one lump sum payment. The rule that damages are assessed once still applies but since the case of *Kelly v Dawes* (1989) payments can be made in the form of periodic payments known as structured settlements. These were first introduced in the United States and Canada, where they are further advanced. Their inception in this country was made possible by the Inland Revenue agreeing that periodic payments were payment of capital and not income which had certain tax advantages.

The system works with the lump sum being calculated in the conventional way. Part of the lump sum is paid over to the plaintiff immediately. The rest of the payment is used to purchase an annuity from an insurer with payments being structured over a given period which can be for the plaintiff's lifetime or longer if the plaintiff has dependants.

Advantages of structured settlements

The main advantage is that the periodic payments are free of tax in the plaintiff's hands. The payments are treated by the Inland Revenue as an 'antecedent debt' and are therefore treated as capital rather than income and are not subject to income tax. Contrast this with the investment income from a lump sum which is subject to income tax.

There are also financial advantages for the defendant's insurer. As structures involve the insurer in greater administration costs, they also argue that they are entitled to a share of the resulting tax benefits to the plaintiff, they are able to negotiate a discount on the lump sum, which is usually between the range of 8–15%. It has been argued that a discount in excess of 8% makes structured settlements unattractive as they are likely to be out performed by investments. This view has been criticised on the grounds that it overlooks the value of the certainty the plaintiff has in knowing that his periodic payments are secure.

They are useful in cases where the plaintiff would be unable to manage a lump sum payment. They also lead to the plaintiff escaping management and investment costs of investing a lump sum. This better reflects the situation the plaintiff would have been in if the tort had not been committed than a lump sum payment, as a regular income avoids the stress of financial management and does not need then the presence of financial experts to ensure its continuance.

The income derived from the annuity is protected from the vagaries of the inflation rate or wild fluctuations in the stock market.

There is flexibility in the creation of the structure. The parties can decide the proportion of the lump sum payment that is to go into an immediate capital payment and how much is to go into the structure.

They ensure that the payments will not cease during the plaintiff's lifetime. A lump sum payment can be dissipated by the plaintiff either through being spendthrift or through ill advised investment or because a prognosis as to life expectancy proves to be incorrect with the plaintiff living longer than has been anticipated. Regardless of the manner in which the dissipation occurs, the plaintiff will become a charge on the State when it is the aim of the compensation system to avoid this happening.

The Law Commission in its Consultation Paper No 125 identified other advantages as they encourage early settlement, thereby saving time and costs and provide certainty for the plaintiff. Early settlement reduces the stress of the litigation process which has proved to be harmful to the plaintiff's rehabilitation.

As they provide the plaintiff with an income, they better fulfil the aims of compensation compared to a lump sum payment as they actually substitute what the plaintiff has lost. They provide income in place of lost earnings.

An advantage for the State is that the defendant is much less likely to claim welfare benefit. It also creates less pressure on the legal system as it promotes early settlement of claims and it ensures that the compensation is used for the purpose for which it is intended.

It improves the image of the compensation system. Instead of the insurer handing over a lump sum to the plaintiff and washing his hands entirely of the case, the replacement system ensures provision is made for the rest of the plaintiff's life. In this sense, it is a more humane system.

Disadvantages of structured settlements
As the amount of the structure is only assessed once, they do not solve the guesswork involved in the assessment of damages. The Law Commission in their Consultation Paper said: 'The pressure to get it right at an early stage is extreme.' It is still possible for the amount of damages to prove inadequate due to an incorrect prognosis. The Pearson Commission recommended a system of structured settlements which would be reviewed in the light of deteriorating financial circumstances, this would get round some of the problems relating to guesswork but the proposal has not been adopted. To a certain extent, all compensatory systems are subject to a certain amount of guesswork. Even a fully reviewable system of periodic payments still has to be based on assumptions relating to promotion prospects, etc.

A further disadvantage is that the operation of the structure is not very flexible. Once the structure is established, it cannot be changed. If there is unforeseen demand for capital, the structure will not be able to accommodate this need. This contrasts with the degree of flexibility which exists at the time the structure is created when the parties can decide how much will be given in immediate capital payment and how much will go into the structure. For a minority of plaintiffs, the loss of freedom and discretion as to the manner in which the lump sum should be invested is a serious disadvantage.

At one time, the plaintiff was subject to the risk that the insurer could become insolvent. Following the Law Commission's Report No 224, the plaintiff is now protected from failure of the life office. Structured settlements have been brought within the Policyholders Protection Act 1975. The Secretary of State can guarantee 'directly funded' settlements such as those by NHS trusts.

The system may simply replace 'compensation neurosis' with a different form of neurosis. The plaintiff may perceive his dependency on the monthly cheque as making his position analogous to a welfare recipient.

The system increases administrative costs and imposes a long term financial obligation on the defendant.

If the question is looked at in its wider context, then it can be seen that as tort victims are already generously compensated in comparison to those who receive compensation outside the tort system then the system in the words of Michael Jones make an 'elite group even more elite'.

Structured settlements do not alter the fact that the system is predicated on compensating the plaintiff for what he has lost rather than on what he needs. By alleviating some of the difficulties associated with the lump sum system, structured settlements may simply be postponing a more fundamental reform of the compensation system.

Limits to structured settlements

Structures cannot be used in all cases and certain limits have been placed upon them.

Both parties must consent to the structure. It was held in *Burke v Tower Hamlets AHA* (1989) that the defendant could not be made to make periodic payments against its wishes.

A structure cannot be imposed after the parties have formally agreed settlement or obtained judgment for a certain sum.

To preserve a structure where a case goes to trial, s 2 of the Damages Act 1996 enables the court with the consent of both parties to make an award under which damages are wholly or partly paid by periodic payments.

A structure cannot be imposed where provisional damages are sought nor where interim damages have been awarded.

It cannot be used in very small claims as administrative costs make it uneconomic.

They cannot be used where there is no liability, for example, awards made by the Criminal Injuries Compensation Board (CICB), despite their decisions being subject to judicial review.

So far, structures have only been awarded in cases of personal injury involving very high awards of damages and it is doubtful whether they will be extended into other areas. Structured settlements are now used much less frequently than in the past. Several reasons have been suggested for this, including the House of Lords decision in *Wells v Wells*, the global economic climate and radical changes in procedure and practice in civil cases introduced in 1999.

Structures are not available for special damages but are reserved specifically for general damages, that is, those damages which cannot be calculated precisely, including future loss.

Damage to property
Where property is completely destroyed, the measure of damages is the market value of the property at the time of destruction.

In *Liesbosch, Dredger v SS Edison* (1933), the plaintiffs were unable to recover where they had incurred additional expenses, as they were too impecunious to hire an alternative vessel while theirs was being repaired.

More recently, hire costs have been allowed in *Martindale v Duncan* (1973) and, in *Motorworks Ltd v Alwahbi* (1977), it was reasonable for the plaintiff to hire a Rolls Royce, while his own Rolls Royce was being repaired.

Where property is damaged but not destroyed, the measure of damages is the diminution in value, normally the cost of repair.

Mitigation of loss
A plaintiff has a duty to mitigate the damage that results from the defendant's tort. But, no wrong is committed against the defendant if he fails to do so. In *Darbishire v Warran* (1963), it was said that the plaintiff is 'entitled to be

as extravagant as he pleases but not at the expense of the defendant'.

Injunctions

An injunction is an equitable remedy and is, therefore, discretionary. A prohibitory injunction is an order of the court requiring the defendant to cease committing a continuing tort. As an equitable remedy, it will not be awarded if damages would be an adequate remedy.

Mandatory injunctions are not granted so readily as prohibitory injunctions; there must be a strong probability that very serious damage to the plaintiff will result if withheld.